END

"I remember years ago whe...
book idea in her living room—she has so much wisdom and insight that I don't even know she fully realized the gift that she is to the Body of Christ. She has been an inspiration to so many over the years, and I am excited to hear the testimonies of encounters that I know are bound to come rolling in once people get their hands on this book.

If you're reading this it's because God has something exciting in store for you. You're about to encounter the angelic host at an entirely new level. By reading this book you will receive a new sense of wonder and excitement about angels, our fellow servants of the Lord. You will learn different ways they can reveal themselves to us, the different functions they perform, as well as how we can learn to interact with them and work together to bring the Kingdom of our Lord Jesus Christ on Earth as it is in Heaven.

This book carries with it an impartation of something that Margie lives out—how to interact with and engage with the angels, those who have been sent and assigned to us to help us manifest God's plans and purposes. Don't set this book down! Instead, get ready for angelic encounters!"

Michael C King,
The Kings of Eden

"Intriguing! Captivating! Amazing angelic encounters are shared with us as author Margie weaves us through experiencing the creative ways God sends His ministering angels. There is no limit to what God can do and how He expresses His heart of love to us. Margie and I have experienced amazing angelic activity at the same time and the encounters and teaching she brings to you in her book are a must read! You will find yourself expectant, having your eyes and ears opened to God's supernatural angelic realm that He desires us to understand and participate in."

Tyler Johnson
One Glance Ministries

"Angels Sing, But Do They Dance? God's Intriguing Assignments For His Heavenly Messengers," is a powerful invitation to go deeper in your relationship with the Holy Spirit and embark on adventures with God's angelic hosts. Margie Moormann lays a strong Biblical foundation for angelic encounters and shares her own experiences. She shows us what is possible in the supernatural realm and encourages us to embark on and engage in our own encounters.

Margie's testimonies of the creative ways God engages with all His creation will inspire you and leave you wanting more."

Debbie Kitterman

Founder, Dare2Hear Ministries; founder, Sound the Call, LLC.; international speaker; pod caster; pastor; blogger, Dare2Hear.com; Dare2Hear The Podcast; D2Htraining.com; author, Legacy: The Lost Art of Blessing, The Gift of Prophetic Encouragement: Hearing the Words of God for Others, The Gift of Prophetic Encouragement Bible Study: Living a Lifestyle of Encouragement, and Releasing God's Heart Through Hearing His Voice.

"This book, "*Angels Sing, But Do They Dance*?" holds nothing back. It unapologetically dives deep into the heart of angelic visitations, giving us an extraordinary glimpse into the unseen realm that exists all around us. The encounters herein shine light into the hidden mysteries surrounding these magnificent creatures and the roles they play as ministering spirits sent forth to serve those who will inherit salvation.

With pure simplicity, Margie Moormann gives the reader practical keys for unlocking the potential of angelic encounters in your own lives. You will find yourself glued to the pages as you read through her first-hand experiential accounts. She unpacks remarkable truths of how these heavenly beings are commissioned to labor alongside us."

Cheryl Fritz

Founder. Inside Out Training and Equipping School

"Oh how the angels rejoice in our salvation! This book wonderfully defines the role of angels in the life of the believer, and contains many of this gifted author's glorious angelic realm encounters. As you read these encounters may your increased awareness of the supernatural ministry of angels bring an increased excitement and expectation. May you personally experience and fully appreciate their divine purpose, as we function in the ministry of the glorious gospel of Jesus Christ!"

Eric Skidmore, Pastor

Grace Center Houston

"Mamma Margie has been a dear friend of mine these many years. She is a passionate lover of Jesus and of every person she encounters. I'm so delighted she is finally able to share in print some of her many and varied experiences with the angelic realm. Each of her stories is a witness which testifies to the goodness of God and of His desire and design for us to partner with his ministering spirits. The encounters invite us to likewise experience the angelic and to collaborate with them in the gospel. I know this book will encourage your love walk with God and will stir up a desire to partner with His angelic ministering spirits."

Christopher Gaston
Owner/Artist
CMG Design Studios

"Margie Moormann is an angel magnet! I have the honor of calling her my spiritual momma and have witnessed the angelic around her. In her book "*Angels Sing, But Do They Dance?*" Margie retells her heavenly encounters with passion drawing the reader into each of her experiences. She beautifully captures the heart of Papa God and his desire to help all his children. As you read these stories a hunger will rise up inside to have your own adventure with the angelic."

Lisa Perna
Host. Touched by Prayer and Crown Chats
Author. Touching the Father's Heart Through Prayer

"There are many books that are written about angels. But I think this book makes a difference from others in regard to the author's many real experiences of angelic encounters. She sees and talks with angels in her real life. This book will make you realize that angels do not only exist, but that we are able to talk with them and be included in their heavenly assignments! It is my prayer that readers of this book, including myself, will experience angelic encounters as the author does."

Kazuko Onishi
Okayama City, Japan

"Wow! This is so much more than a book – it is an interactive experience with God! As you open your Bible and read the scriptures alongside Margie's teachings and stories… each chapter becomes like your own personal discipleship session in how to see into the heavenly realm. Margie then gently and effectively opens the curtains and doors of your thoughts and your knowledge of the scriptures – and shifts your understanding to a whole new experience of God's life and interaction that is around your every day. Your walk with God, and your awareness of the Kingdom of God, is going to be taken to new levels through this book… Thank you, Margie!"

Tom D. Schermitzler
Pastor/Guest Speaker, God's Living Room

In the opening pages of this revelatory book, Margie Moormann makes the statement "We are coming to a time when our responses will be similar." She is referring to the common angelic activity during the time of Jesus. Angels are among us and are ministering beings sent by the Lord to help us and reveal His nature and character to us. As she shares her many personal encounters in the angelic realm, take the time to read and respond to the Points to Ponder and the Prayers. The personal revelation and increased awareness of those among us will hopefully bring you into your own personal encounters. The emphasis is not on the angels as much as on the increased relationship with "Papa God" and His deep love and goodness for each of us. I believe Angels Sing But Do They Dance will open your eyes, as Elisha prayed for his servant. It's a must-read for the days we are in and are coming into! I am excited to see this book spread across the ecclesia in the nations!

Sande Lofberg
Aglow International
US Director Great Plains Rocky Mountain Region
Associate Pastor Destiny Four Square Church Rapid City SD

ANGELS SING

BUT DO THEY Dance?

God's Intriguing Assignments For His Heavenly Messengers

Margie Moormann

ISBN: 9798367148725

Scriptures with bolded portions are to express emphasis by the author. Please take note that the name of satan and related names are not capitalized. The author chooses not to give him importance.

Cover design and book layout by Tracy Buzynski. Celebrating Design.

DEDICATION

In thanksgiving, honor, and praise I dedicate this writing to my Heavenly Papa God who opened my eyes to see.

Understanding the angelic realm is not essential for life in Papa God, Jesus Christ, and Holy Spirit. But it does make it quite extraordinary!

FOREWORD

Margie Moormann and I had the pleasure of meeting several years ago at a gathering where the miraculous things of God were being valued and taught. It does not escape me that those who attend such gatherings absolutely believe what the Bible tells us, and further believe that we can indeed have a close, personal relationship with the Lord. I also am one who believes that everything the Bible shares with us is for us. Margie and I share that same certainty.

In my eyes, it tells me that we are headed in the same direction because I believe that in addition to actually knowing God, we have access to miracles which should be normal for those in Christ, as well as signs and wonders and seeing in the Spirit which is for all believers. Angelic visitations can be everyday life as can the many other supernatural things too numerous to list here.

Over the last several years, Margie and I have spoken and shared testimonies with each other about visitations with God and encounters with angels. These visitations and encounters are something that we both experience a lot. I am repeatedly excited to see God visit people in this way because true visitations of God will always change people and cause them to become more Christ-like. It is quite a blessing to witness that transformation as it occurs. Much in the same way that Margie shares encounters in the realm of the Spirit with me, she shares them now with you. "Angels Sing. But Do They Dance?" reveals not only Margie's life and walk with God but also what God has waiting for you! These encounters and angelic visitations are a powerful example of what one's life will look like if we have a desire to know God in this way.

Strongly supported by scripture, I believe we see how the Lord is glorified in these encounters as we read this book. Angels will never accept the glory or honor when we speak with them, and we see that these personal encounters do not cause us to be drawn to the teller of these things, but rather be drawn to the Holy One...The Lord Jesus Christ, who has captured the heart of the author who shares these events with us.

I highly recommend this book "Angels Sing. But Do They Dance?" I know you will be blessed, encouraged and impassioned in your walk with the Lord!

Michael Van Vlymen
River of Blessings International Ministries
Author. International Speaker. Teacher. Artist
riverofblessingsinternationalministries.org
michaelvanvlymen.wordpress.com

CONTENTS

ACKNOWLEDGMENTS

I lift a hallelujah to my Lord and Savior Jesus Christ! He has brought awesome people into my life. With so much to be thankful for I am expressing my deepest appreciation and gratitude to the following people for their invaluable contributions making this book endeavor a reality:

First to my amazing, loving, giving, unselfish husband Lew. You protect and support me, love me always, are trustworthy, dedicated, encouraging and a strong steady shoulder for me to lean on or celebrate with through all the victories and trials we have experienced together. We've always known God is with us. You generously give of yourself, your knowledge, your skills and your resources every time and place there is a need. Thank you that you have given me the often-needed essential times of laughter and craziness, and by the way, the marbles are still there. I am thankful for your understanding, patience and grace to me as I took on this long overdue writing process. Thank you for giving me space to meditate or write, even when you had no idea why I was retreating. I am grateful that we share our lives in Jesus, having grown so much in Him, always seeking to learn more. I thank God for Him knowing before we did, that we were meant to spend our lives together. I continuously thank God for you and am loving you forever.

To our precious family, Eric, Kristi, Jeffery, Jenna, Marci, Kevin, Kylee, Scarlett, Prescott and Briar Grace thank you for your constant love, compassion, caring and the bubbly joy and wisdom you all carry. I love the games we play, the questions we raise, the conversations we have, the prayers we pray. You are a gift and blessing to me right from the very heart and character of our loving God, and to Him I am eternally grateful for you. The twinkle in your eyes constantly lights up my world! Forever my hugs and kisses are to you all. You are cherished, adored and loved by me and by Jesus. He wraps you in His love and carries you in the palm of His hand. I love you with my whole heart.

I am blessed beyond measure to have you, Carol Anderson as my bestest, forever friend. You are such an inspiration to me. I describe you as my friend who is just like Jesus! You always love as Jesus loves, you're encouraging, compassionate and you honor others above yourself. I'm thankful we speak God's truth to one another, agreeing in prayer and believing that with God all things are possible. Thank you for cheering me on with your uplifting words, and for praying as this new God-happening was before me. The angels are truly an incredible visible part of our friendship. I am thrilled and thankful that we share so many memories throughout our life-long, friendship. We know God has so many more plans for us to experience.

Barbara McCullough, you started this journey with me. We shared new unexplored supernatural experiences, were excited to ask Holy Spirit questions and to understand the deep meaning of what we were experiencing. Our constant response to every encounter was always "Wow, God, Wow! Thank You Holy Spirit." We couldn't define or identify exactly what was taking place, but we were elated, thankful and full of bliss. Those were fabulous days of learning, growing, encountering, sharing, seeing, and hearing in what we called our unchartered, unfamiliar waters with our Papa God. We dove deep into Papa God's ocean of revelation. Thank you for walking side by side with me then and now. I thank God for your friendship, for being able to share the angelic encounters with you, and for our intense love of God expressed through Jesus that we have in common.

To my PGH confidante, Karen Arias, who is always only a phone call away. You and I have walked through exciting times together as we discover unending diamond-like facets of God's love and how He commands His message-carrying angels to serve us. We explore and discuss at length (even into the wee hours of the morning) His visions, angelic activities and words that have been delivered by His angels to us. Thank you for your agreement with me to never stop discovering the spiritual and supernatural unknown. Your excitement for the plans of Papa God yet to be accomplished is marvelous! Anticipation builds each time we talk. Thank you for your gracious giving heart, for committing yourself to Papa God's Hideaway Ministries, and for your prayers and the loving go-for-it encouragement with this book. It has boosted my energy and priority many times. I appreciate you. Thank You Jesus for my special Sync Sister.

A huge thank you to my Papa God's Hideaway Ministries Focus Team and the PGH family that keeps growing. Your belief in, support of, and anticipation of our times together in Him exemplifies the excellence of His gatherings. He has shared His announcement of profound importance that we are to move forward with Him and you all are willing. Thank You Lord God, that my team has recognized Your ministering angels during our awesome, holy times together. I give thanks to You, Holy Spirit for showing and directing us in the upcoming new calling Papa God has for us. May we continue to exalt the name of Jesus, name above all names and recognize the assignments God has given the angels concerning us.

To my God-Stickers ladies, Ann Stevens, Minda Scherer, Brenda Rather and Nancy McKenzie. God has placed us as His stickers in His treasured sticker book and He has only begun to draw the background scenes for each page we are in. What exciting eye-opening adventures He has taken His GS girls on. Thank you for trusting me as your mentor in the beginning, and for being open vessels so willing to be filled with Him. Papa God has awesome plans for each one of you and I'm excited to hear of and watch them unfold.

To the numerous groups around the world who are seeking more, and invite me to speak at your engagements, I extend my heartfelt thanks. Even years back, when this walk in the spiritual realm was first being experienced, you trusted my sharing in your yearning for knowledge and encounters. Meetings with you all are amazing. As those of you that have, and those that will witness the presence of the angelic host, hear the angels' songs, absorb the teachings, step into the supernatural realm, and celebrate your new discoveries, my spirit rejoices! I look forward to more blessed times with you.

To my trusted friend, Michael Van Vlymen, thank you that we have a shared excitement of angelic and our supernatural encounters. I honor you! Papa God must be planning an over-the-top engaging conference for us together, because we have talked about it for years now, but yet to have it manifest. We are waiting, Papa God, believing that You must be putting all the perfect pieces into place. Michael, I thank you for your confidence in me during our sharing times and for writing the foreword for this book. I cherish our friendship. I speak an abundance of God's blessing and goodness over you. I thank Jesus for putting you in my life.

To all my spiritual sons and daughters and to those of you in my mentor groups who call me 'Momma Margie', I'm clasping you in my arms, hugging you and thanking God for each of you. You've been in many visions and words given to me by Papa God. May God's angelic realm become your normal life as you partner with God and His angels. I am blessed by your spiritual yearning, growing and commitment to experiencing who God is, the spiritual realm that we live in and the Kingdom of God within you. Thank You Lord, may You keep pouring revelation, understanding, wisdom and the knowledge of You into each one seeking more.

Lisa Perna, you are my amazing spiritual daughter and I am blessed! Your faithful, constant encouragement, your heartfelt love and prayers for this project, and the "there's no stopping you now" declarations you spoke caused me to follow the rhythm of Holy Spirit's leading and finish this writing. It seems we know a song for everything and the Christian song that claims "we won't stop now" is one I had been singing as the angels celebrated each step of the way. I'm grateful to Jesus for the incredible adventures you and I have taken together and the many adventures with Papa God yet to come. Loving you! May God keep blessing you big with every spiritual blessing in the heavenly place.

To Karen McCune who was the first person to publicly post on social media that I should write a book, bless you Karen. I am convinced you were speaking to me from the heart of God. And to Dave Hayes who endorsed the idea publicly for years, many thanks Dave. Seven years is not so long, right? Michael C. King, Tyler Johnson, Debbie Kitterman, Cheryl Fritz, Eric Skidmore, Christopher Gaston, Lisa Perna, Kazuko Onishi, Tom Schermitzler and Sande Lofberg, I am grateful for you and appreciate your time to read and enthusiastically endorse this book.

To Michael and Sunshine King for sitting with me in the living room discussing, recording thoughts, assuring me that the subject of angels is something people would want to read, and giving me the nudge to put together many of my angelic encounters. Thank you for your friendship, wisdom, suggestions, knowledge and prayers!

To the book team that Papa God chose and put together for me, I cannot express enough gratitude and thanksgiving for your help. You individually and together are astounding to me! The success of this book comes from your steadfastness, insight, respect and diligence.

Debbie Kitterman, did you know what you signed for? What a super coach and friend you are to me. Your practical, innovative, honest, ongoing suggestions, ideas, confirmations and striving for perfection kept me moving, although often not fast enough. Your acceptance of my lack of technical skills, and knowledge of all the components needed to put together a book are beyond awe-inspiring. How you were willing to allow me to lean on you, to rely on you through thick and thin times is remarkable. Thank you for keeping my doubts at bay and your unceasing enthusiasm always ahead of my thoughts. Your steadfastness is awesome. You are definitely number one, Debbie! Thank you so much my friend. We did it!

Amy Udager, you are a hidden gold nugget! Thank you for your scrupulous dissecting and editing of this book. You are incredibly wise, respectful, humble, helpful and conscientious. Your suggestions, presented in positive fashion, the way you honed in on my manuscript in such a timely manner, the knowledge you carry of scriptures, and your disciplines in so many areas are extremely impressive. Because of your faith in God, you understood His vision for this writing. I am eternally grateful to Papa God for leading me to you for this project. You and I burst out laughing many times and reverently blessed God more times along the way. Your enthusiasm for the finished product allowed me to sleep and not be wide awake with concern during the night. You bring joy to my heart, and blessings to this project. I thank Jesus for you.

Tracy Buzynski, you are a gift from God! He knew I didn't have any idea how to proceed with asking someone to create a book cover for me. But then, the first time we were in a meeting together I watched as He held out His hand in front of you and said to me "ask her." What a blessing you are! You are an amazing, diligent, tenacious cover and layout designer. You were careful to discern my desires of the message I hoped to convey with the cover design, and to show me many options. We both celebrated when the final cover came together. We knew it was once again the hand of God. Your insight of formatting the book, your computer skills, and you providing a smooth read is a gift well received. Thank you so very much for believing in the contents of *"Angels Sing, But Do They Dance?"* Your sincere guidance and professional work made this book beautiful to look at and a wonderful reading experience for my readers. Thank you Tracy. I love and appreciate you.

I would not have been able to complete what God asked me to do over seven years ago without these professional, humble, knowledgeable, gifted people who flowed into my life as God's token of love. We can now proclaim in unison it has been done! I am deeply indebted to you all, and want once again to express my deep appreciation and sincere thank you to each one of you. Well done!

And to all my readers, thank you for your enthusiasm to explore the contents of this book. May you be inspired to seek out and answer Papa God's personal invitation to you. *"The grace of the Lord Jesus Christ, and the love of God, and the fellowship of the Holy Spirit, be with you all"* (2 Corinthians 13:14 NIV).

And especially to Papa God, Jesus Christ and Holy Spirit, thank You for taking my hand and showing me the wonders of Your Kingdom, of the spiritual realm over which Jesus reigns as King, and the joy of living and engaging in the supernatural kingdom of God. It's because of You that my heart cried out to share these encounters with the readers. Worthy are You Lord.

"Not to us, O Lord, not to us, but to Your name give glory because of Your loving kindness, because of Your truth"
(Psalm 115:1NIV).

Angels Sing But Do They Dance?

GOD'S INTRIGUING ASSIGNMENTS FOR HIS HEAVENLY MESSENGERS

Has the question "do angels dance" piqued your curiosity? You may have heard a few people report about occasionally hearing angelic voices singing. But do angels dance?

I'm excited and eager to share the answer with you as your reading adventure continues. I haven't seen them doing the two-step line dance yet, but if God desires to give the message of His awesome love for us through angels dancing, I am assured the angels dance perfectly. And they don't need lessons! Through numerous encounters with the angels of God over many years, I've witnessed them doing surprising things while completing their supernatural assignments from our Father God.

We give God the praise, honor and glory for His care of us. Angels do not act on their own accord, but are servants, ministering spirits of our Most High God. They carry out the voice of God assigning them to serve those who will inherit salvation. They have always been, and will continue to constantly be around us. In both the Old and New Testaments angels play a key role in God revealing Himself to us. Angel appearances were so common in the lives of the New Testament Jewish people, that when Peter was told by an angel to leave the prison, he followed the angel out, and went and knocked at Mary's house where many were gathered. The servant, being assured upon hearing Peter's voice, ran to tell the other occupants of the house that Peter was at the door. Now here's the proof of the commonality of angels in that day. The friends emphatically told her she was mistaken. It was not Peter they said, it just must be his angel! They, however, understood and accepted the familiar activity of angels. We are coming to a time when our responses will be similar.

Angels are not to be worshiped. Only Father, Son and Holy Spirit, our Three-in-One God is worthy of our worship. We are allowed and able by God's providence guiding us in our journey of faith, to participate and partner in His divine angelic activity.

Are you curious how angels that are sent by our Father God often appear to minister to us? I'll relay some amazing angelic encounters I've had during multiple years from the past to the present. But first, here's my back story.

As a young wife, seems like eons ago, my love for and relationship with God intensified and I began calling Him Papa God. This endearing name for Him sang out from my heart. Papa God stepped in shortly after and had me discover that He speaks to us all in His creative ways. I have realized that along with the infallible word of God, Papa God also uses angels, visions, experiences, and supernatural perceptions to bring an understanding of what He is saying to me. As I was beginning to comprehend some of His creative ways of communicating with me, this awesome, impactful experience happened.

I was walking briskly down a sidewalk in the neighborhood I grew up in. Getting outside, early in the morning to catch the fresh breeze and hear the birds singing is a wonderful start to the day. Stately houses set on green grass hillsides faced the street. As I walked by one house I noticed a large picture window with a Queen Anne wing-back style chair setting to the side of the window. Seated in the chair was a man seemingly enjoying the morning hustle of people headed to work or delivering children to school, and me, the passer-by on my morning walk. Looking up and glancing again at him at the window, I smiled and waved a "good morning." Time to hurry on. He pleasantly waved back. Only a few feet into walking further I heard an audible voice, emphatically and lovingly stating "Don't just pass me by. Come and sup with me!" What? Where was the voice coming from? No one else was taking a walk at that time. That comment seemed to be a serious one. I had heard a few people say that they had experienced the voice of God, and had read in the Bible that God frequently speaks audibly, but hearing a voice when no one was around was new to me. Inquisitively I looked back at the window. The man's appearance had changed. Light was radiating from him, and I felt an incomprehensible love coming from his gaze. As my entire body reacted to this pure, magnificent light, my foot deviated to the right a bit and caused me to stumble, but I managed to catch myself before falling. I was new to this kind of experience, but truly Jesus was speaking to me! I was not in a church service.

I was on a morning walk in my neighborhood. Immediately I became so overwhelmed with being wrapped in the glory of the moment that I gratefully responded under my breath as I kept walking "Yes, Jesus. I will definitely come and sup with you."

All I could respond to Him was YES! I was ready to be in a place I had never been with Him before. I was ready to leave the familiar church system I had known and experience the new territory He was offering me to tread on. I was eager to spend time with Jesus, listen to the words He would speak, to be wrapped in His glory, to understand the fullness of His Kingdom, and to be filled with the joyous sounds of praise. My YES touched His heart and was what He wanted to hear. With that one word I spoke, my continuous years of amazing, endless, supernatural encounters began.

If you're ready, I'm ready to share some incredible experiences of cooperating with the promptings of angels, and how they carry the message of the unending, unconditional, extravagant love Jesus has for each one of us. These encounters are not in any chronological or specific order. They span over thirty-five years and are an illustration of one of the numerous ways Papa God communicates with us, sharing what's on His heart.

I'm praying that you can peruse the encounter stories with anticipation, excitement, expectancy, and the revelation knowledge that Papa God wants each of us to partner with His angelic force. God never gives up on any of us. He loves us so much that He continues to use even His angels to draw us into His marvelous Kingdom family. No matter where you have been or where you are now in your spiritual walk, Love Himself is calling your name with an awesome invitation to attune your spirit to His magnificent angelic realm!

"Bless the LORD, ye His angels that excel in strength, that do His commandments, hearkening unto the voice of His word"
(Psalm 103:20 KJV).

There is a story of a dog that was chained to a tree. He ran around and around the tree, making a familiar path. He wore the path deep. One day a passer-by came along, felt sorry for the dog, and set it free. The dog ran a little way, but then came back so he could run around the tree. The chain was off his neck, but not off his mind. We don't want to keep walking down the 'known path'. We know what happens there. Let's go for the unknown path. Allow God to move sovereignly in, on, and through you. Participate in what He is doing! He's a good Papa God who desires to speak to us.

A religious principality locked the gate to the angelic realm hundreds of years ago. In the New Testament, it was a normal part of life for people to engage angels. Our Greek rationalism thinking got in the way and we dismissed the reality of the angelic realm. But God is returning the mystery of the Kingdom back to His body in this day.

Understanding the angelic realm is not essential to our salvation. In the glorious nature of God there are no limitations as to how He reveals Himself to us. Peter says in his writings that the angels are intrigued by salvation and long to look into the things concerning salvation (1 Peter 1:9-12 NIV). Understanding the angelic realm is a bonus for us as we walk this extraordinary life with Papa God, Jesus and Holy Spirit.

God created a society and culture with angels. Angels have free will and as the word of God tells us, some rebelled against God and are considered fallen angels who submitted to their own pride. However, God loves, speaks with and is surrounded by the myriads upon myriads of angels who love and serve Him. Jesus converses with the angels, and we can too. They are in the spiritual realm and that realm is within the space we are occupying, wherever we are.

The apostle Paul addresses the existence of angels and of their power and influence. He also reminds us that we too often focus only on what our natural eyesight comprehends, but that the angels are at work all around us whether seen or unseen.

Angels are mentioned over 300 times in the Old Testament and the New Testament. The word 'angel' comes from the Greek word 'anglos' which means messenger in Hebrew. These messengers were created by God, continuously worshiping and glorifying God the Father and God the Son! They are subject to the Word of God and sent out by Him as ministering spirits.

Papa God calls his angels "holy" and "mighty". Mighty is the word dunamis which means dynamite, inherent power. But did you know dunamis is not just dynamite but rather EXPLOSION! The angels release the energy of God, excelling in strength (Psalm 103:20 KJV).

They will war against the demonic forces on our behalf (see Daniel 10:13 KJV; Revelation 12:7-8 KJV). The angelic forces carry the assignment of God and the anointing of the Kingdom of God.

There is much to understand about angels. It is astonishing to comprehend how active and involved God's angelic beings are in our lives and the Kingdom.

They are an intricate part of God's Kingdom. God's angelic messengers impart teaching, healing, wisdom, guidance. Angelic beings reveal God's love and comfort, His plan for us, His plans for His Kingdom. God never disagrees with His word as He sends us His message.

Angels sit in heavenly councils, or courts (Job 1:6 NIV, NLT). They are able to eat food. (Psalm 78:25 KJV). Have you experienced how they can bring answers to prayers? (see Acts 12:5-10 NIV). Angels will encourage us, equip us. Sometimes, curiously, they get very expressive and just want to have fun! Angels experience joy, and having personality characteristics that impact how they behave or feel (Luke 15:10 KJV).

Angelic beings cannot be everywhere at the same time. They are not omni-present, but are sent by God anywhere He desires. God created them to carry and operate with much power but they are not all-powerful as God Almighty is. And God is not their father (Hebrews 1:5 NLT). They refer to Him as *I AM*, the very name God called Himself when talking with Moses (Exodus 3:14 KJV).

The hosts of angels cannot make decisions to do assignments on their own, and are not to be worshiped (see Revelation 22:8-9 NIV). They know the grandeur and holiness of God and are in constant, unceasing worship and adoration of Him. Angels have the ability to appear as men when God assigns them to deliver His message (see Daniel 10:5-6; 16; 18 NIV). Our eyes see what is in the natural, but we now can also see with spiritual eyes because of the power of Holy Spirit in our lives. Whatever and however God directs them, the angels appear and respond accordingly.

If you've had encounters with angels, use each experience to ask for more. The more we engage the clearer things become. Each supernatural and angelic encounter we have will bring revelation of the awesomeness of God, the magnificence of Jesus and the beauty of Holy Spirit. We are all carrying the message of the Kingdom of God! It's time to understand more of the supernatural realm and magnitude of activity going on within it.

Have you acknowledged yourself as an ambassador of God's Kingdom, one sent by God as His official representative? God's angels honor ambassadors. Consequently, when you honor (esteem, respect) the angelic realm, angels show up. The Presence of Christ and the manifestation of who He is, is always accompanied by the angelic. That's the reality of the Kingdom.

Angelic beings are fascinated by our view of Jesus. Jesus is the Lord of the angelic host. They will always be drawn to where we are worshiping and glorifying Jesus and lifting up His Name. Know with certainty that as you worship Jesus, in whatever form that may be, throngs of angels will be surrounding you, actually drawing you close to the Throne, to be worshiping together with God's holy angels.

Every story you hear about divine angelic visitation carries a seed to open that realm over your life. There are no rules to follow! Our creative Father God is not limited by what we think guidelines must be. Often, Papa God will instruct the angels to orchestrate the "coincidences" that occur in our lives, showing God's glory.

Papa God shows us more facets of Himself each time He sends a messenger angel. He made us with a sense of humor. He often shows us His. We can relax and believe that He enjoys communing with us in numerous ways. He's such a loving Papa God who knows each of our personalities! Each one of us is made in His image and He is crazy in love with us!

There is an order, or a divine hierarchy of God's angels mentioned in the Bible.

- Michael is an archangel, the commander of God's angelic armies, a protector.
- Gabriel is an archangel and entrusted messenger.
- Raphael is also an angelic messenger.
- Cherubim are associated with holiness and were placed at the entrance of the Garden of Eden after man sinned. They were also on the Ark of the Covenant.
- Seraphim are the six-winged angels who sing God's praises without ceasing. The four living creatures are an exalted order of cherubim, continuously in motion around the Throne of God.

Names are important. An angel's name dictates his character and reveals his mandate and the role he plays. Scripture mentions:

- Gabriel, his name means "God is my strength."
- Michael, "Who is like God."
- Raphael, "God heals."
- Uriel, "Light of God".
- Remiel, "Mercy of God" "Thunder of God."

Some of the names of angels I've encountered are:

- Pathfinder
- Extreme
- Elyacaph, "God has added. God increases the family."
- Risata, "Laughter, Joy."
- Rakak, "Tender, Soft."
- Amos, "To Carry."
- Zavad, "David."
- Perception
- Ezer, "Help, Support"
- Deliverer
- Nahal, "To Lead."

I have forgotten at times to ask their names, and I regret not questioning them. God is offering us an invitation to see clearly the supernatural and angelic activity of His Kingdom! He is longing to introduce us to new places in the heavenly realm because He wants us to partake in them! Angelic encounters provoke us to step deeper into our relationship with God. A large number of us have come from a "theology only" background, not an experiential one. However, everything is spiritual and has its origin in the spirit of God. The angels have always been since God created them, but are now being 'detected' because we have spiritual eyes open to see.

"Don't be afraid," the prophet answered.
"Those who are with us are more than those who are with them." And Elisha prayed, "Open his eyes, LORD, so that he may see." Then the LORD opened the servant's eyes, and he looked and saw the hills full of horses and chariots of fire all around Elisha"
(2 Kings 6:16-17 NIV).

There is no formula or format to follow, only a desiring heart. My friend Michael Van Vlymen gives a suggestion of an exercise to begin seeing angels. "Sit in a room when it is just beginning to get dark. Focus on the bit of light that is still in the room. Concentrate on it and expect to see movement. As you do this, more and more clarity will come to you".

You may see movement, colors, lights, shapes, or human forms. Angels have no uniform or inherent visible appearance because Papa God has them show themselves to us in ways that will be best for our understanding of the assignments God has given them. You may feel a touch, smell a scent, hear a sound, and even experience a taste letting you know an angel is close. I started on this incredible journey by seeing moving, colored lights. The more I received, believed and realized they were angels, the more they intensified. Throughout the years the heavenly messengers have manifested in various forms, including seeing them as a person sitting next to me at a table.

Father God is rich and colorful in the way He interacts and communicates with us. He meets the expectation of our hearts and spirits. God will use whatever form He chooses to speak to us. He is not a silent God.

I value the angelic realm. I wonder if I would interact with the angelic realm if I didn't value it. However, I had to open my mind and heart to learn. I was not brought up understanding that God's angelic realm is always profoundly active in our lives. Someone said, "We can materialize the word of heaven on earth when we speak of what we see or what we hear." I pray my sharing will be a tool to deposit into your spirit a deeper revelation of the divine facets of our holy God's glorious Kingdom.

God is raising your level of expectation!! Trust the small things, He'll give you the bigger.

Thank you for letting me share some of my angelic encounters with you. They are testimonials of one of God's many creative ways in which He constantly showers us with His abundant love. There is always so much more to learn and experience in this amazing journey of life with Papa God. He is eager to have you join Him on a journey specifically designed for you.

May I pray a prayer with you? You are invited to read this prayer aloud.

Father God, thank you that You love me with an incomprehensible love. I want to be in Your presence to know You better. Heighten my awareness of the supernatural realm I live in, and of Your angelic presence. Let me fully understand that Your angelic realm is just one of the many amazing ways You help me grow into the fullness of the knowledge of Jesus Christ and the Kingdom of God.

I ask You to awaken my five senses of seeing, hearing, smelling, tasting, and touching to the knowledge that they are supernatural senses, and not just physical senses. Shake them, wake them up to the truth of their function. Cause my body, soul, and spirit to respond to the senses which have now been awakened. Cause me to see or perceive the heavenly realm of the spirit, and to receive what it is that You, Father God, are showing and telling me.

I thank You for Your unending extravagant love for me. Our Father in Heaven, hallowed be Your name. Your kingdom come, Your will be done, on earth as it is in heaven. Amen and Amen!

Dear Reader,

Are you ready to embark on an adventure with me into the supernatural realm and activate angelic encounters in your own life?

Allow Holy Spirit to minister to you as you read each encounter. Allow Him to open you up to the wonderful supernatural realm and angelical encounters.

At the end of each encounter, you will find two sections, "Points to Ponder" and "Prayer." "Points to Ponder" were designed to help you process each encounter personally and to take you into a deeper revelation of your own. The "Points to Ponder" are not only for the individual to pursue. They may be useful for group contemplation, research and discussion. The prayers are for you to read aloud to activate each encounter in your own life.

I encourage you to take your time as you read through the encounters. Engage in conversation with Holy Spirit regarding how you can experience your own angelic visitations.

Remember, there is always more to learn and experience in this amazing life adventure with Papa God. He is eager to have you join Him on a journey specifically designed for you.

Enjoy your journey! May you experience God's amazing love and greatness.

Blessings,

Margie

ENCOUNTER

Rattling the Spiritual Realm

Listen! Can you hear the angels gathering? Are you recognizing the rattling and rumbling noise of extreme movement and explosive activity in the spiritual realm? Are you realizing the massive angelic battalion waiting to be released to do combat over cities and governments throughout the world?

Papa God is directing His angels to respond to His word spoken through the prayers, decrees, and declarations of His people. Your intercession throws out the nets into the sea of humanity, and into the sea of established governing bodies of nations, states, communities, and organizations.

What happens when He pulls the nets in? Explosions! Expect to see and hear more explosions of His Glory! One by one nets are being pulled in. Keep interceding. You're doing exactly what Papa God wants you to do. You are an awesome, valued, integral part of the people of earth under the reign of our mighty, Holy Father God, Jesus Christ His Son, and Holy Spirit.

You are taking the heights like the eagles. You are flying in the heavenly realm where He is releasing spiritual adrenaline, piercing eyesight, and the revelation of 1 Corinthians 2:9 within you.

Keep on keeping on! God hears you and knows the spiritual conflicts that are working against His holy plan. Your prayers move God to send out His angels. His angelic battalion is deployed, well-established in warrior skills, and is responding to God's command at a moment's notice.

"For the eyes of the Lord are on the righteous and His ears are attentive to their prayer" (1 Peter 3:12 NIV).

Escalation in the heavenlies is happening! Change is taking place as you pray. A turning from wickedness is happening. His Throne is established on righteousness and justice. The righteous will have much to celebrate! God is restoring lost time (see Joel 2:25 KJV), restoring a right relationship with Him, renewing purpose to the nations and communities of peoples, giving revelations of identities, creating new life, and *bringing about His good plans and a hope for the future* (see Jeremiah 29:11 NIV).

"But as it is written, eye hath not seen, nor ear heard, neither have entered into the heart of man, the things which God hath prepared for them that love Him" (1 Corinthians 2:9 KJV).

Points to Ponder

- Have you sensed there are battles over cities and governments?
- Are you anticipating a result?
- Do you join the band of intercessors praying for your nation, community and all governing forces?
- Is the thought of interacting with angels new to you?
- Ask the Lord to give you discernment, guidance and favor as you seek to know His plans for you in encountering the angelic realm.

Prayer

Father God, as Your beloved, allow me to grasp how intensely the angels fight on my behalf and how You hear and cherish each one of my prayers.

Angelic Energy

Oh my! What is that bone-jarring rumble coming from far off? Abandoning my inside project, I head outside, hoping to identify the sound.

Looking up into the cloudless sky I see an infinite formation of gleaming lights approaching me at an accelerated speed. These lights appear to be a formation of airplanes, but as they come closer the pronounced presence of angelic energy is almost unbearable. I see them! Hundreds and thousands of angels!

The brilliance of their radiant energy is like having floodlights shining in my eyes. I need to look down and away momentarily. The reflection of the approaching angelic presence is extremely intense.

How did this happen? The rumble has changed to heavy vibrations of a marching cadence. K'dah, k'dah, k'dah, k'dah. The angelic formation is marching in a rhythmic sequence. I'm curious as I note the angels are not compacted tightly together, but each has ample room on all sides.

I've learned while encountering angels that there is frequently a message I am to share. As I watch and listen, Holy Spirit solemnly proclaims "It's time to fall in, take your place and march into the supernatural. You're being catapulted from your former spiritual place and position to your new supernatural positioning to do exceedingly, abundantly above all that you ask or imagine, according to the power that works in you" (Ephesians 3:20 KJV).

There's an electromagnetic energy field everywhere that contains so much angelic energy. It's time to step into the spaces the angels are providing, passionately pick up the supernatural cadence and participate in the effective advancement of the Kingdom of God.

"Being asked by the Pharisees when the kingdom of God would come, he answered them, "the kingdom of God is not coming with signs to be observed, nor

will they say, 'look, here it is! Or 'there!' for behold the kingdom of God is in the midst of you"
(Luke 17:20-21 ESV).

Points to Ponder

What would your life looked like if you heeded these scriptural words today: "It's time to fall in, take your place and march into the supernatural. You're being catapulted from your former spiritual place and position into your new supernatural positioning to do exceedingly, abundantly above all that you ask or imagine, according to the power that works in you."

- What does it mean to be Jesus' shining light?
- What former spiritual place have I been in?
- What is the Lord saying your new position looks like?

Prayer

Father God, Thank You for Your deep love and affection for me. Allow me to see myself the way You see me when I am not able to see it personally. I know I am called to be Your shining light. Help me to walk in this truth, and step into my new supernatural position.

ENCOUNTER

Heavenly Doors

Mornings often present themselves as a perfect time to be in the swimming pool, soaking up the warmth of the sun, listening to my favorite worship songs, and enjoying the stillness of the early daytime hours.

"Okay!" The word resonated in a boisterous, emphatic manner. It seemed someone was speaking through a megaphone. I looked up and around, expecting to identify where the voice was coming from. "Okay!" came the word again. Several voices echoed in unison.

Looking skyward I questioned aloud. "Excuse me?" My dog, who was lying lazily on the patio, abruptly sat up and barked at the silence being broken. Steadily my eyes searched for the source of the repeated word I heard.

"Okaaay" came the word one more time. The inflection in the voice sounded playful. It was time for me to get out of the pool and investigate.

As I climbed out and sat on a bench with my feet dangling in the pool water, an angel appeared and sat beside me. "Take a look," he said as he raised his hand. An unexpected wind caught the leaves on the trees and momentarily blew our way. From just above the tree line in our yard, many angels lowered themselves to a standing position around the edge of the pool, seemingly at attention, and waiting for a command to be given. My eyes quickly scanned these angels. Their bodies varied in shape, height, and weight. Many appeared quite muscular. I was surprised as I looked closer to realize there was a wispy, iridescent film of light coming from within each one. The pool water began to dance with sparkling waves of joy as brightly shining sun rays hit the water and the light from the angels mirrored the sun's reflection.

Shocked at seeing so many angels present, I inquired of the angel. "May I ask your name?" I hadn't thought to question him before, but it seemed important. "Pathfinder" he replied. "Why are all of you here?" "We are constantly with you. Your home is a habitation of angels. *I AM* has given us an assignment of ministering to you, helping you to get to the right place at the right time. You have not been aware of us before," he told me. He took my hand and I felt a wind beneath us carrying us upward past the stratosphere, the planets and beyond into open space.

As I gazed at the awesome wonder encompassing us, I was surrounded by an infinite number of heavenly doors in every direction I looked. There was no end to the doors and no gap between them. They were on top of and beside one another. None had handles to push or pull the door open. Every door was sturdy, large, open, and inviting me to enter. Inside each door was a poster hanging on a wall. A poster? How strange. What am I to do with a poster?

I waited for Pathfinder to tell me to go ahead and seize the poster hanging inside each door I might enter. But instead, he told me my instruction from *I AM* is to take the poster from only one specific open door. "How do I know which door?" I asked. "This is the one" I heard.

Entering the open door before me, I grabbed the poster off the wall and came out to where Pathfinder was waiting for me. "Now we are to head back," he exclaimed. I questioned him with my eyes. He continued, "What is written on this single poster is extremely important for you to understand."

With the poster rolled up and slipped under my arm, Pathfinder and I instantly arrived outside my home on the bench beside my pool.

"I will be staying with you while you discover what the poster says," Pathfinder cheerfully told me. I interpreted the tone of his comment to mean he was as curious to find out as I was. Carefully unrolling the poster, I read the word printed on it.

"Membrane."

It sounded like Pathfinder gasped in astonishment. Or maybe it was excitement. I was thinking that membrane was a metaphor. I had once heard instruction from Holy Spirit that I was to come into agreement with a particular metaphor. "What does Papa God want me to understand from seeing this word?"

Pathfinder calmly advised me to tell him what came to my mind when I heard the word membrane.

Trying to remember from biology class, I told him, "Membranes cover or separate various parts of the body. The cell membrane allows some substances to pass through it but also prevents others. I know the skin is a membrane. There are defense membranes that cover organs keeping them from friction if they bump into other structures in the body. I recall that each membrane has different characteristics and functions. The body responds to the coverage and protection they bring."

"Do you hear what you are telling me?" Pathfinder inquired. Suddenly, I felt I was struck with inspired insight.

"Oh! Holy Spirit always points to JESUS! Papa God had me find and open only this poster because JESUS CHRIST is the true membrane holding the Body of Christ together! He is our defense against the discord. He is our protector and the one necessity which will hold us through any trial or storm. He wants us to not be discouraged by what we see with our eyes, or hear with our ears, but to look to Him and see what He is doing in the spirit realm."

"Yes," Pathfinder responded. "And *I AM* desires that His body understands that you need each other. You are each an integral part. Build each other up. Speak to one another with words of encouragement. There is untapped potential in everyone. Set your minds on the eternal picture."

"Thank you, Papa God, for taking me to this special heavenly door." Pathfinder's gentle smile agreed. "Let the love of Jesus and the mind of Christ be foremost in your lives."

I was not able to see Pathfinder or the other angels leave, but I was confident they are with me always. I would be ready if they came again to take me to the open heavenly doors.

"Of the angels He says, "He makes his angels winds…"
(Hebrews 1:7 NIV).

"After this I looked, and there before me was a door standing open in heaven. And the voice I had first heard speaking to me like a trumpet said 'Come up here'…"
(Revelation 4:1 NIV).

"While we look not at the things which are seen, but at the things which are not seen; for the things which are seen are temporal; but the things which are not seen are eternal"
(2 Corinthians 4:18 KJV).

Points to Ponder

- What does the word membrane mean to you?
- Have you ever felt an unexpected slight wind and pondered if it was an angel?
- Have you allowed yourself to consider that because you are a child of God your home is a habitation of angels whom *I AM* has given assignments concerning you?

Prayer

Lord God, bless me with understanding and allow me to experience Your comfort as I rest in Your promise that Jesus is continuously holding all things together in my life.

ENCOUNTER

Heavenly Doors A Second Time

"Why are you waiting?" A voice behind me questioned as I stood by my kitchen sink. "Why am I waiting for what?" Quickly turning I saw the familiar angel Pathfinder who often makes himself known to me. I had the feeling he had quietly been there for quite some time. "Waiting for me to show you more doors" he answered.

"Oh! I'm always ready for more." I talk with him as I do a friend who is enjoying a cup of coffee with me. He knows my language. Nothing complicated, just to the point. "Let's go then. Come with me." He was eager to do God's bidding. "Okay. I'm ready" I enthusiastically told him.

The angel put his hands on my shoulders. A wind briskly brushed over me. I quickly turned my head glancing to see he was still behind me. The liveliness and joy on his face was undeniable. He appeared thrilled to answer the call from Papa God to take me with him.

"Do you remember the time you were in the unknown space that was filled with nothing but open doors?" he asked. "Oh yes, of course, I do. I will never forget it. Quadrillions of doors that seem to endlessly go on and on."

He continued to converse with me. "You informed friends that there were so many open doors continuing indefinitely. I know what you did when you entered one door, but give me the details."

"Well, I grabbed a poster which hung on a wall inside a door. I tucked it under my arm and you had me read it."

In a thoughtful manner he mindfully stated "*I AM* was pleased watching you as you pulled the poster off the wall, realizing it and others held treasures you would discover later." I attempted to assimilate the incredible words I heard. Treasures? I wondered how long it would be before I discovered the heavenly treasures.

My eyes shut momentarily. When opened I saw we were in the middle of the sea of doors again. There was no floor, no ground to stand on. Pathfinder and I were suspended in air. A feeling of breathlessness came over me and I wondered if there actually was air to breathe here.

My comprehension of this expanse of open space was so limited. I concentrated on the endless number of doors. Each door was tightly positioned next to the another. My mind recalled being here and moving inside a few open doors while gathering the one poster hanging on a wall inside each door I entered.

I began to retell the angel Pathfinder of the quadrillions of doors that surrounded me last time. He cast a broad smile my way. Continuing to share the experience with him, I related that I was allowed to read only one.

Pathfinder encouraged me to go ahead and enter more doors and unroll the posters I found. "Tell me what the posters have written on them" the angel inquired. I looked at him in shock and surprise. "Are you helping me find new paths that Papa God has set before me?" He didn't answer directly but lifted his arms upward, lowered his head and reverently proclaimed in a loud voice "To God be the Glory!"

I explained that each of the posters I unrolled had only one word on them. The first poster said *'Bereavement'*. It puzzled me and caused me to wonder if a tragedy was forthcoming. But Holy Spirit had me research the word and I discovered bereavement is the time we spend adjusting to a loss. Pathfinder listened intently as I shared my experience of giving up my years of Old Covenant thinking, and embracing the New Covenant that Jesus died to give me. "It is an adjustment," he agreed "to lose, even willingly, a major part of your former spiritual life." "Yes!" I responded, recalling how I had progressed quickly into grasping the magnificent gift of righteousness I now have because of Jesus.

"The second poster read *'Perspective. My Eyes Are On You'*. I know Papa God is telling me to encourage whoever I can to have His heavenly view of everything, with His true perspective instead of what our flesh comprehends and evaluates. His eyes are on all of us, taking care and loving each one with unconditional Daddy love."

"Poster number three read *'Metaphor,'* Isn't that odd, Pathfinder? Metaphors are symbolic. But I heard once that a metaphor is the crowbar by which we pry open the doors to truth and life. We are to come into agreement with the metaphors." Leaning forward with what seemed like a sly wink Pathfinder commented "and you are one who is so visual and has so many symbolic encounters. Come into agreement with them! *I AM* is holy! Doors will open to more truth and to an even greater life."

"He is magnificent, glorious, majestic, amazing, almighty, and powerful. I cannot adequately express my love of Him." Pathfinder squeezed my shoulders in a comforting way. "I understand." His kind words were singing Papa God's song of tender love into my ears.

Pathfinder gently said "You will gather more posters, but regardless of how many times I bring you here, you will never go through all the open doors and never find all the posters. Get what you can. Remember, they are treasures for your heart."

"Okay" I answered. With that, we were back in my kitchen. His hands lifted off my shoulders. He was invisible.

"What we have received is not the spirit of the world, but the Spirit who is from God, so that we may understand what God has freely given us."
(1 Corinthians 2:12 NIV)

Points to Ponder

- Have you been through a season of bereavement or adjusting to a loss?
- Can you recall an opportunity when you may have encouraged someone else by sharing God's perspective?
- Has anyone encouraged you in that same way? If so, journal about it.
- What metaphor might open new doors to truth and life within you? Can you come into agreement with it?

Prayer

Father God, adjusting to loss is hard to do alone. I pray You will open doors of understanding and revelation to me. I also ask that You draw me close to Your heart and release Your tender love.

ENCOUNTER

Endless Open Heavenly Doors

Pathfinder apparently had an extensive assignment from God. Once again, he took me to the endless open heavenly doors. I automatically knew what to do, and gathered a poster hanging on the wall inside each door I entered.

My eyes focused on a specific door. An invisible sign on the door reading 'transition' welcomed me in. I took down the poster hanging on this wall understanding it was unmistakably there for me to seize. It curiously became rolled in order to be preserved and I easily put it under my arm as I proceeded through the next open door. Moving rapidly into door after door, collecting posters off each wall, I was tempted to count how many were under my arm. The number would confirm how small an area I covered each time I had been here. I stopped momentarily to gaze at the view of infinite doors, never completely grasping what must expand billions of light years in every direction.

Pathfinder smiled his approving smile, and asked me if I was tired. I told him I felt no sensation of being tired. He chuckled. I know he laughed because in the spiritual realm there is no time or physical limitation.

"What posters have you collected" he asked. I started to take them out from under my arm to unroll them. He put his hand on the posters and stopped me. "You will open them, soon" he advised me.

In the blink of my eye, he and I were back in my home where I first heard Pathfinder talking to me.

I engaged him in conversation and told Pathfinder I felt as if I had been attached to an arrow, catapulted with accelerated speed towards God's target, the poster. "Yes," he said. "*I AM* is reminding you He is the archer, you are His arrow. His plans for you are not secret. They are deep within your heart. The posters are revealing His plan in a way He knows will have a gripping effect on you." Instantly as he spoke, I heard many voices singing, '*It is the glory of God to conceal a matter; to search out a matter is the glory of kings*" (Proverbs 25:2 NIV).

"Pathfinder, who is singing?" "It is the company of those who are surrounding and guiding you as you have totally submitted yourself to the Kingdom School of *I AM*, His Son Jesus and Holy Spirit." Listening as he explained who and why the company of angels was singing, I felt adrenaline surge through my body, and became acutely aware of my own shallow breathing. In a response of overwhelming awe, I affirmed what he told me, shouting "I am internalizing and manifesting the teaching of the King!"

Pathfinder let me catch my breath, then instructed me. "Now unroll the posters from your first trip through the doors." They appeared in front of me. One by one I unrolled the six.

Poster number one read *Uncompounded*. "Oh! Free from the mixture of Old Covenant and New Covenant teaching for His church! No mixture regarding the truth of who and whose we are, and free from disorder! No more cultural discrimination. Instead, we live in the pure, perfect nature of Almighty God." Pathfinder nods.

Regeneration was written on the second one. "It is a power-packed word pointed at revitalizing the gifts within myself that have become dormant and forgotten. Regeneration reconnects me to the deep things in the mind of Christ for the purpose of His Kingdom".

On poster number three I saw the word *Invasion*. I told Pathfinder it sounded like a military term. But my spirit understood that it indicated taking back the occupation of areas once seized by the enemy. This is exactly what Matthew 11:12 in the Amplified version says,

> *"From the days of John the Baptist until now the kingdom of heaven suffers violent assault, and violent men seize it by force [as a precious prize]."*

My spirit was rejoicing! Preparation was being made in the heavenly realm as well as within the body of believers for her to possess her rightful place!

Number four poster read *Confidence,* speaking to me of complete trust and belief in who I am in Christ. I am one with Him. With confidence I am empowered, strengthened, and engaged in Kingdom living.

Extension was written on poster five. The Body of Christ is coming into a time of limitless understanding of our true identity and authority in Him. I told Pathfinder it made me think of God's word in Isaiah *"Enlarge the place of your tent, stretch your tent curtains wide, do not hold back; lengthen your cords, strengthen your stakes"* (Isaiah 54:2 NIV).

The last poster I have had the word *Quest* recorded on it. "Be in constant pursuit of obtaining all that is available to you," Pathfinder whispered. This adventurous expedition with Pathfinder was amazing! I am grateful that he was leading and guiding me. "Holy Spirit is with you and will lead you into the time and the teaching within all posters. He is your connection between the seen and the unseen realms."

"Does this mean you will not be taking me back into the vast expanse of open doors?" A twinge of sadness came over me. Pathfinder answered me, "My joy is doing as *I AM* assigns me. Remember the voices that sang His word to you? I am part of that company."

With that he stepped aside and was not seen.

Sitting in my chair, communing with King Jesus, I thank Him for His grace, His outrageous love, and for this tremendous encounter once again. I know I have many more posters yet to be unrolled, and a burning desire for more of that which only God can provide.

In an instant I hear soft angelic music from a heavenly choir responding to my praising Jesus. This soothing, melodious music fills every portion of my home as the wondrous love of Jesus poured over me.

I know who is singing.

"Are not the angels ministering spirits sent to serve those who will inherit salvation"
(Hebrews 1:14 NIV).

Points to Ponder

Imagine finding and unrolling one heavenly poster with a word written on it. What is the word you see?

- Describe the thoughts that come to you as the word is revealed.

- Do you sense a strong message when you see the word?

- Visualize what the message may entail? Describe.

Prayer

Lord God, wrap me inside Your heart and help me to comprehend the rightful place I have in Your Kingdom.

ENCOUNTER

Unobstructed View

Flying 39,000 feet in the air on a cross-state flight suggested I get my book out and start reading. It was mostly quiet on this flight other than a few rows behind me with the voices of two relaying their upcoming business appointments.

I was enjoying the calmness of a smooth flight and no deep concerns invading my mind. "Good morning, ma'am." The gentleman seated in the seat next to mine continued. "How are you this morning?" "I'm doing well, thank you." "Are you on a connecting flight?" he asked. "Yes, I have a short layover." I took a quick glance at his rugged facial features and wondered what he would be doing at his destination. "Where are you headed?" I asked him. "I catch many planes and go where I am called," he replied. "May I ask what book you are reading, ma'am?" I showed him the cover and expressed what wonderful insights are tucked inside. He nodded. "A very well-written book."

I was able to continue to read for a good portion of time. The silence was broken mid-flight as the cabin crew offered snacks and a drink for the second time. My coffee and water choice was perfect.

"Excuse me" the gentleman began. "I am wondering what you notice out there?" He raised the window shade and looked outside. Leaning forward, and tucking my book in the seat back pocket I questioned him. "Am I looking for something specific?"

"Well, take a look and tell me what you see." Hesitantly I agreed and glanced out the window ready to report what I saw. "There is a large city but I'm not sure which one we are passing over. Some scattered billowy clouds are moving below us."

"It is beautiful, isn't it?" he remarked. I assured this man who was instructing me in a strange way that I agreed with him. "Sights from this altitude are often breathtaking. I really enjoy the stunning scenes we are able to see from the planes. Soaring mountains are my favorite" I added.

"Why is that?" He questioned. "Because they are the majestic masterpieces of our creator God. And I think how all things were made of what was not visible. It's awesome to contemplate that."

He lifted his head, seemingly focusing on one section out the window and asked, "Do you see activity out there?" Being questioned in such a way, I was certain there must be something he saw and wanted me to validate.

I looked up, down, and as far to the sides out the window as I could. And as I did, God alone, who is the source of my spiritual eyes, allowed me to see three very tall muscular angelic forms positioned at the end of the wing span behind us. They were in a standing position, with no floor or structure under them. Their broad shoulders touched each other's. The three angels appeared to be standing still, yet moving at the same speed as our plane. I was weighing the option of telling the gentleman this sight I perceived when I felt led to announce "I believe in God, Holy Spirit and my Savior Jesus Christ."

"Yes, I know you do," he replied. "I knew as I observed you board this plane."

"That's interesting. What made you know that?"

"I have constant communication with your Father God."

Responding to his comment, I felt the sweet spirit of God and said "He is wonderful to talk with and listen to."

"Yes," he replied. "He is holy."

"Did you see there are three angels traveling with us?" I asked, curiously questioning if he was aware of them.

"Yes. I was assured you could see them also. I was directed to encourage you to look."

I desired his authoritative answer when asking him, "are they watching over this plane full of passengers?"

"They are tending to their assignment," he replied.

That wasn't specific enough for me. I questioned him a few times but was not able to get details, only a slight smile from him.

This was an unexpected, unusual flight I thought to myself. Papa God had once told me that I had been launched into exciting experiences with Jesus, Holy Spirit and Him.

I wondered who this man was. I remained silently deep in thought for quite some time. Not knowing what direction our conversation would take next, I asked him if he would be able to talk while I wait for my connecting flight. He explained that there would not be much time to spare and he would have to hurry to his flight. I understood and thanked him for the compelling experience he shared with me.

As we were preparing to deplane, he stood in the aisle, looked at me still in my seat, and commented "on your next flight ask the flight attendant with the short brown hair about her daughter."

How did he know what my specific connecting flight was? I entered the jet bridge only a few people behind him, wanting to ask him one question, but suddenly he was nowhere to be seen. I believe he was an angel on his precise assignment from Father God, and absolutely I will ask the flight attendant about her daughter.

Points to Ponder

"Do not forget to entertain strangers, for by so doing some have unwittingly entertained angels"
(Hebrews 13:2 NKJV).

- Are you aware of a time or times when you may have experienced this scripture? If so, what reaction did you have?

- Describe the encounter.

Prayer

Papa God, I pray You swing the doors wide open for me to walk into the amazing activity of heaven.

A Flip Chart

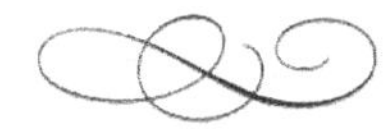

A small group of believers is desiring to gather in prayer. We meet for the first time together, for the purpose of getting acquainted, expressing our beliefs, and sharing a few prayer experiences. Feeling comfortable sharing concerns, we begin to pray. I notice a large angel in the corner of the room with a flip chart of papers on a tripod easel. He is holding a pencil and records each prayer and petition that we lift up to our God. One of our concerned members seeks the Lord in prayer to change a disruptive message that is being given at church. I explain I see an angel, and he is writing down the exact words that are prayed. Angelic activity is new to most in the group. But it's just like Father God to send His angel as a scribe, assuring us that God hears every concern in our hearts and every cry in our souls.

The following weekend the message of the church had completely turned around as was petitioned. Angels may appear as scribes, or in any form God chooses.

"For the eyes of the Lord are on the righteous, and His ears are attentive to their prayer…"
(1 Peter 3:12 NIV).

Points to Ponder

- Are you aware that the Lord hears you as you speak of Him to or with others?

- Find the keywords in this scripture.

"Then those who feared the Lord spoke with one another. The Lord paid attention and heard them, and a book of remembrance was written before Him of those who feared the Lord and esteemed His name"
(Malachi 3:16 ESV).

Prayer

Father thank You for always hearing every concern of my heart and the cry of my soul. Forgive me for the times I thought You weren't listening.

AN INCREDIBLE ENCOUNTER OF DIVINE LOVE

Most of All Love

My favorite comfy chair wraps its cushions around me. It is the perfect time for communion with Jesus. Gratitude sweeps through my spirit as I worship Him. I feel a gentle touch on my hand. Jesus also loves communing with me yet the energy in the touch indicates it's an Angel saying "Come with me. Here we go."

With my eyes closed I yield to His words. Time stands still. I sense the atmosphere has changed and open my eyes to see I am in an enormous cathedral. It is much larger than photos I've seen of St Paul's Cathedral or Westminster Abbey in London. Where am I? The location doesn't matter, I am just being shown how immense this cathedral is. Hundreds upon hundreds of worshipers can be seated I tell myself, noticing the almost endless rows of pews in the sanctuary.

The angel directs me to an aisle seat close to the back. The pews fill up with people quietly anticipating something unique.

Studying the details and the beauty of the interior of this cathedral takes my breath away. It is magnificent! Gold shimmers as glorious bright lights flash throughout the massive space. I want to reach out and hold in my hands the tangible, thick light. This must be a very special occasion.

I hear whispers from the people behind me. Turning to look towards the entrance to the sanctuary, I see a father walking his gorgeous bride down the aisle. Thank You Holy Spirit for bringing me to witness a ceremony of profound love!

As the father and bride walk towards the waiting groom, people are putting their hands on their hearts. Astounded, guests gasp seeing the bride. Each is declaring emphatically "Oh! That's me! The bride looks just like me!"

Light radiates from the bride as she and her father approach my aisle. I'm aware of her exquisite beauty and the love her father has for his daughter. She is not walking with her arm through his, nor are they hand in hand. He is holding her hand up in a position similar to the beginning of a waltz. The father-daughter dance has begun. I am looking at her beaming face and I am astonished as I too recognize myself in her. "She is me!" I exclaim.

They continue walking towards the waiting groom. Only a few more steps. But just before the bride reaches her beloved, she stops and shouts out "Wait! Please! I understand it now! There's more! Wait!" She turns and quickly moves down the aisle, exiting outside. Abruptly I get up and follow her.

Once outside the cathedral our eyes are opened to an unexpected sight. We both see many homeless, hungry, hurting people. The angelic being tells me they have always been there, completely unnoticed. With clear vision I see people in deep ditches, in gutters. Many are yelling "Don't judge me!" Voices are crying out in agony from all over. Frantic ones pull at the bride's dress as she comes near them. Her dress is being shredded as they reach for a piece of what they perceive she has. Empathy rises within me as I feel the bride's compassion and love. I hear her tell the hungry people there is food prepared for each of them inside. She touches their heads with what seems to be power released from her hands. As she does so, their dirty, torn, foul-smelling clothes change to radiant, shining, fresh garments. Eagerly they head inside the cathedral to eat a much-needed meal.

The bride walks toward a steep hillside, her feet slipping down into a deep, dark abyss with dense, tangled undergrowth. I am with her, understanding the mission that has overtaken her. Countless despondent people are caught in the undergrowth, groping to find something to hang on to that will pull them up, but to no avail. They are too weak, unable to get to the light above on their own. These living souls are barely surviving in the dark blackness. They are not even able to cry.

Pulling one unrecognizable body up the hill and placing this person of amazing value and worth in a safe place, she is determined and yells "Help me!"

Wedding guests begin to vacate the cathedral. Soon the building is emptied. Guests have responded to her call. Her groom appears at the door smiling broadly, acknowledging he afore knew what was going to be transpiring.

Feeling empowered, I link arms with the bride. Others link arms, connecting us with each other. We are now one with the bride. She becomes larger as we bond as one, each of us knowing the assignment we are called to complete.

Our unified body is so large that in one step we lower ourselves to the dark chasm below. Six people at a time are being rescued. Working diligently, we breathe a breath of thanksgiving as all who were once in the pit are now lifted up into the light.

More curious people arrive. They react to the rescued ones before them, holding them, loving them, affirming them.

Wedding caterers with their hands and arms full, bring the entire elaborate meal outside, arranging it on the ground to serve all who have congregated. Those who were radically transformed are now serving others.

Everyone has joyfully settled, sensing a calm which has replaced the chaos. Eating together, being nourished at the makeshift banqueting table is awesome. I witness an amazing phenomenon happening. The sky is ablaze with a spectrum of vibrant colors. All eyes look upward. All ears are hearing joyful singing and celebrating as angelic voices respond to what has occurred.

The air feels cool. Small gentle raindrops fall on those that were downtrodden, broken, hopeless, and alienated. Their heads now are lifted high, arms extended to the heavens. They have been completely restored. Uninhibited, as if scenery and people had dissolved, they break into dance.

The oil of gladness has been poured out. Jubilation has replaced despair. God's heavenly messenger whispers that I am witnessing the manifestation of the Kingdom of God. We indeed are one body united as the bride. He explains that together we have become a company of billions around the world.

"Look what I found!" someone excitedly yells. An enormous, weighty sign with the letters L.O.V.E. Is being drug behind him. All are excited and grab an edge of the sign. On the count of one…two…three we toss it into the air. Up, up it goes. Gravity is not pulling it down. Angels must be holding the sign. It has taken over the sky. All of creation has got to be able to see it!

My attention is drawn to the father of the bride who has been standing back observing all that has taken place. A brilliant spotlight of gold shines on him. His awesome love, pride, joy, and adoration of his daughter permeates the atmosphere as he walks towards his daughter.

Everyone is watching as he gives his daughter a gentle hug, kisses her sweetly on her cheek and with strong, penetrating emotion in his voice he announces for all to hear "THAT'S MY GIRL!"

We come together, unified in His Spirit and know that Papa God is saying "and most of all, Love." My awesome experience is over. I'm back home with my heart and spirit full.

"Now you are the body of Christ, and each one of you is a part of it" (1 Corinthians 12:27 NIV).

"...as a bridegroom rejoices over his bride, so will your God rejoice over you" (Isaiah 62:5 NIV).

Points to Ponder

- Have you heard the call for help and answered it? If so, recall the experience and write about it.
- If not, was there a time when you wished you had?
- What emotions rise within you in both instances?

Prayer

Lord God, may I know and experience my worth and value in You. Allow me to feel Your passionate love that beams with pride for me.

ENCOUNTER

Water Table

It's Thursday, one of the days each week I can occupy a church classroom by myself. This private room presents me with an exceptional opportunity to worship, study, pray and hear from Holy Spirit.

In the room adjacent to mine I hear a group of women laughing heartily. Laughter is good medicine. It is delightful to hear this jovial expression of them enjoying the day. My heart is happy also.

Desiring a cup of java this morning, I begin to pour the coffee from my thermos. I'm looking forward to my first cup and my conversation with Jesus. A notebook and pen are ready to record what He shares. He and I enjoy our time together as we discuss the events of the day ahead. His Presence and His love permeate the room. As I take that first sip of coffee, I am startled by the sound of the heavy classroom door being thrust open.

Standing in the doorway is a tall angel, the size of the doorway itself, bearing a sign hanging from his neck which reads "Water." He doesn't move until I pull out a chair and motion for him to come in and sit down.

"May I ask why you are wearing that sign? Is that your name?" Without saying a word, the angel flips the sign over. On the back are the words "Table Rising." "The water table is rising, there is a sound like a thousand waters" he tells me. It surprises me, and my mind reverts back to the summer when the hurricane deposited 50" of rainfall in our city. A feeling of uneasiness comes over me as I hear this phrase. "What does that mean?" I ask, hoping to hear something other than the warning of another flood.

"*I AM* is saying the water table of the nation and church is rising. He has set in place before each of you divine choices to be in on the cutting edge of what *I AM*, Jesus His Son, and Holy Spirit are doing." My apprehension shifts to anticipation. "*I AM* is raising up sons and daughters with a supernatural awareness of their destiny, birthright, and oneness in Jesus. Not one is being left out."

These are powerful words. I'm writing in my notebook as fast as I can hoping to include all that he is saying.

I look at my hands and see some oil pooling in the palm of my right hand. "What is this for?" Questioning the angel in my mind while observing the oil, I feel Holy Spirit has told the angel my thoughts. He looks seriously at me and proclaims "The body of believers will see and hear the explosion of Glory. Each of you is a carrier of His Glory. "

I think of how we live in the light of God's presence and release a shadow formed from His light.

"For it is the God who commanded light to shine out of darkness, who has shone in our hearts to give the light of the knowledge of the glory of God in the face of Jesus Christ"
(2 Corinthians 4:6 NKJV).

We have the presence and power of God overflowing from us. Pondering this verse and concept prompted me to ask "are our shadows dangerous to the enemy?" It may be a silly question, but I am serious. He replies to my question, "The Body of believers in Christ will invade cities and nations with the immeasurable power and presence of *I AM*."

As I recall back only a few years it seems there has been a dramatic change in the focus of fellow Christians desiring the supernatural strategies, mandates, and scepters of government that are being given out. I have an understanding that no longer will we ask, "Is this me? Or is it God?"

The angel continues, "The accuracy of knowledge within God's people is becoming precise. The passionate believers are not doubting their identity in Christ, their spirit of sonship and inheritance, or their potential. They have moved into an era of greater Kingdom authority. Solutions from the Triune God are in their DNA. The devoted Bride has the mind of Christ."

I'm talking to myself, but realize the angel is listening. "The truth of our identity in Christ was never shared while I was young and growing in Jesus. It is crucial that we comprehend we are one in the spirit with Jesus. I am thrilled this teaching has risen to the forefront. Hearing

Papa God calling us mature in our understanding is exhilarating. We are vigorously experiencing His revelatory realm and the supernatural places in God."

The angel speaks into my thoughts. "*I AM* wants you to know that the believers' thinking has shifted into a declaration. They declare the words of God with certainty, clarity, confidence, and conviction. Now believers are stepping into their rightful place, bringing the Kingdom of God to every ground where they set their foot."

He turns towards me, opens his mouth, and with a booming voice proclaims "Listen, believe what you have inherited. These promises are yours to be taken boldly. The time is now! The ground does not give way underneath you. You are stepping into the solid, strong, unwavering Kingdom authority which has always been yours."

"Yes!" I agree excitedly. The angel walks to the door, saying "Hear the heart of Jesus beating with love as He watches the Bride of Christ express His love to the world."

The door opens and he exits. I forgot to find out his name.

I have such eagerness and expectation in me! I feel the motion of our advancement! Papa God, the Host of Heaven, and the Cloud of Witnesses applaud with thanksgiving as we believe and move in who God says we are! No more doubting or delay. We have eyes and ears wide open. We are seeing Heaven's design.

What an invigorating, beautiful time hearing the words of Papa God through the angel this morning. The water is rising, and the Bride of Christ is dancing and jumping for joy in the waves of His Glory.

"Let them praise His name with dancing and make music to Him with timbrel and harp"
(Psalm 149:3 NIV).

"Who has known the mind of the Lord so as to instruct Him? But we have the mind of Christ"
(1 Corinthians 2:16 NIV).

"I promise you what I promised Moses. Wherever you set foot, you will be on land I have given you"
(Joshua 1:3 NLT).

Points to Ponder

- Have you felt your shadow is dangerous to the enemy? If so, in what circumstance(s) has that feeling come about?

- Are you aware you are a carrier of God's Glory? Be specific in naming times when you carried His glory with confidence and assurance.

- Were others aware of the glory?

Prayer

I thank You God that You have called and equipped me to be Your glory carrier and an agent for change in this world. Help me see and hear the explosion of your glory.

SMALL SIGHTINGS

Take The Corner

Sitting outside with a prayer group we see three angels sitting with us in patio chairs. One angel asks the other two. Shall we tell them?" The other two agree. The angel in the middle says, "You are at the corner right now and it is an unfamiliar corner. As you take the corner you will see sights that were unnoticed before. The sights are like a flash before your eyes, causing a sudden thought, insight, or inspiration about what you see. The flash will be intense, bright, and overpowering." Another angel adds, "It will be an incredible turn. Be sure to take the corner. Do not go straight but seize the corner turn. You will now be positioned at the unfamiliar corner and the difficult areas will be overtaken by victories. There will be sights to explore that you have been hoping and waiting for. This corner is the point where the natural and supernatural meet, where your perception is suddenly that of heaven."

The angels insist many times we take the corner. With belief and expectation, we do, and are ready to experience the unexpected.

"Where there is no prophetic vision the people cast off restraint..."
(Proverbs 20:18 ESV).

"Behold, I am doing a new thing; now it springs forth, do you not perceive it?"
(Isaiah 43:19 ESV).

Points to Ponder

- How do you interpret the meaning of the phrase "take the corner?"
- Have you been encouraged to take the corner?"
- If so, in what capacity? Discuss the results.

- Do you sense God is doing a new thing in your life, community, nation?

Prayer

Father God, I am ready to experience the unexpected. Allow me and show me how to take the corner where the natural and supernatural meet.

ENCOUNTER

Presence

I just got off the phone with someone needing prayer support. Thank You Jesus, for Your healing Presence ministering to the needs of Your beloved one.

Now it's time to prepare some dinner. After washing my hands and reaching for the towel to dry them, I hear a faint chuckle. Thinking it was my husband I check behind me, but he isn't there. A soft voice says "don't wipe off the anointing" followed by another chuckle. Holy Spirit, what is this about? I don't even have oil on my hands. Why the faint laughter? Is something pleasing, or is it amusing? Is an angel talking to me?

Okay. I'm listening.

Holy Spirit begins telling me about oil. Shepherds poured oil on sheep's heads making their wool slippery so that lice, fleas, and ticks would not find their way to burrow into the sheep's ears and brain, killing them.

I've read in Biblical accounts that oil became a symbol of blessing and protection. A person was anointed with oil signifying occupations, or callings on their lives. Soldiers, hunters, craftsmen, scribes, priests, kings, and prophets, along with others, were all anointed. In the tabernacle Moses anointed all utensils, equipment and furnishings within the tabernacle to order to set them apart.

An angelic voice clarified "*I AM* says, 'tell my Bride physical oil itself is not the anointing. Your anointing never leaves you. Anointing is His Presence and power residing in you."

Continuing I add, "some would ask about the New Testament verse, '*Is any sick among you? Let them call for the elders of the church to pray over them and anoint them with oil in the name of the Lord*' (James 5:14-15 KJV). The people in that time culturally understood the use of oil as a representation of the Presence of God. Assurance would come from the spiritual strength of those called to be elders."

"Another thing, occasionally we like to use oil as a contact point for the one receiving to sense Papa God's love." I make the comment from experiencing and using oil in this way.

"Yes," comes the angel's response. "Oil is good and often suitable, but not essential for the anointing of *I AM* to be present. His anointing abides in you. The spirit of Jesus Christ the Messiah, the Anointed One remains within you. Witness the undeniable evidence of Jesus' love, the comfort of Holy Spirit, and the complete sonship with *I AM* as you pray with others."

"This seems be that which we already are aware of," I comment to the angel. "I have a feeling Papa God was chuckling thinking how His Bride sometimes gets too fixated on needing to use the method. Apparently, we occasionally need a reminder that conviction of God's power is sometimes given by the procedure with oil. But the manifestation of God's power and glory is through Him who continues to abide within each of us forever. Period."

"What is your name, angel?"

"Ezer." Nodding in agreement I tell him, "You make me smile. Reiterating for clarity is important."

I had to look up the Hebrew name Ezer. It means help or support.

"Now it is God who makes both us and you stand firm in Christ. He anointed us, set His seal of ownership on us, and put His Spirit in our hearts as a deposit, guaranteeing what is to come"
(2 Corinthians 1: 21-22 NIV).

Points to Ponder

- What is the difference between the oil of anointing within you and the anointing oil which is used in the Name of Jesus in prayer, encouragement, consecration?

- What do you think about this statement the angel relayed from *I AM*: "Oil itself is not the anointing. Your anointing never leaves you."

- What thoughts come to you in this statement: Anointing is His Presence and power residing in you.

- Do you believe you are set apart, as a conduit of God's power, and anointed to proclaim the good news of Jesus Christ?

Prayer

I pray, Father God, for the goodness of Your Presence, and the oil of Your anointing to be unmistakably present in me, in my spirit and mind. Be with me as I operate in the fullness of Your Spirit as Your favored one.

SMALL SIGHTINGS

An Angel's Prayer

Our granddaughter at two years old was in the hospital critically ill. For many days we took turns with her parents being with her so she wasn't alone and then rotating. We would find recliner seats in the large family room to spend the nights. During one day in the family room a gentleman approached and sat next to me, asking why I was there. After explaining my granddaughter's health issue he kindly asked if he might pray for her. I don't recall his exact words, but it was a prayer for the peace of Jesus, Holy Spirit's comfort, and Father God's reassurance that our granddaughter would be okay, healthy and taken care of. I was blessed by his concern, encouragement, prayer and declaration. Opening my tear-filled eyes to thank him, I noticed he was not in the chair next to me. I asked the people sitting across from me if they had seen him leave. They mentioned they had not seen anyone in the seat next to me at all. An angel was sent to bring much comfort and peace.

"Praise be to the God and Father of our Lord Jesus Christ, the Father of compassion and the God of all comfort..."
(2 Corinthians 1:3 NIV).

Points to Ponder

- What does the scripture *"Don't forget to show hospitality to strangers, for some who have done this have entertained angels without realizing it"* (Hebrews 13:2 NLT) mean to you?

- Have you had this experience?

Prayer

Thank You Holy Spirit for being my comforter and friend. Thank you for the times You have sat with me and I was unaware. Father God, would you send me reassurance today for the things that concern me.

ENCOUNTER

Swish, Swish

The newly renovated retreat center where I am invited to speak is in a campground setting among tall trees, their leaves dripping with rain droplets hitting the ground. I park my car in the upper level and load my arms with books, papers and even a hot dish I had made to share at a meal we are having together. Carefully navigating my way down the slippery path of cut tree rounds with my arms overloaded and not having clear vision in all directions is not the best idea.

"Do you need help?" one kind attendee asks me. "Oh, thank you. If you'd like to take this hot dish that will be very helpful." Handing her the hot dish causes an unbalance in my standing. As I take the next step, my feet go out from under me and all I can see when gingerly raising myself up from a laying position are my papers and books scattered on the soggy ground. I am surrounded by ladies all helping to retrieve my materials. My clothes, brown with grass which has turned to mud, hair in my face, squished mud between my fingers, and a confidence that is now replaced with embarrassment is all I can offer the loving souls that set me upright. Attempting to walk is a disaster. Painfully I hobble while concerned women place their arms under my shoulders and around my body.

I don't immediately have my leg checked or x-rayed. Instead, I sit in a chair all weekend while giving my messages at the retreat. The chair becomes my closest friend. I use it as a walker to lean on, taking weight off my leg while maneuvering to the areas I need to be.

Arriving home, I am immediately taken to a hospital to undergo x-rays. My tibia and fibula are both fractured as is the radius in my left arm. No wonder I had a problem pushing the chair around that was my crutch that weekend.

My first realization of an angel coming close to me is the night after settling back at home from the retreat. I need to sleep in our recliner rather than struggling to get up and down from the bed. As I am dozing off, I hear the swish, swish, swish, swish of my husband in his synthetic nylon early-age track suit coming down the hallway. I feel him stop at my left side and look over my shoulder checking to see if I am managing to sleep. I smile in response to the warmth I feel and the love I am receiving. Being sleepy, I keep my eyes shut but know he is lovingly making sure I am somewhat comfortable. Swish, swish, swish. He's heading back to bed satisfied that I'm okay. But something seems a little bit out of character. No kiss. No hug. No word of comfort.

I begin to seriously question if an angel was sent by God to comfort me. My husband will always wake me and ask me if I'm okay. But this time, oddly he didn't say anything. I have read many times in Luke, *"He will command his angels concerning you to guard you and protect you"* (Luke 4:10 Amp). I even referenced this scripture during the previous retreat days.

Clicking the chair remote, the leg rest on the recliner drops accordingly. With my leg in a cast and my arm in a sling, I grab the new available crutch beside my recliner and head down the hallway to our bedroom. My husband is asleep. Speaking loudly to make sure he can hear me I ask him if he just checked on me. Surprised that I am standing before him instead of laying in the recliner he answers, "No. You just woke me up."

"But I heard you walking down the hallway," I answered. "I've been asleep" he reiterates. "Are you okay? How can I help you?" "Yes, I'm doing okay. Thanks, but I need to ask God a few things. Good night. Love you. Sleep well."

Hobbling back to my recliner for the night I question Papa God and am now aware that I indeed witnessed God's angel, sent to let me know God is watching over me. I thank Jesus for His love and protection, and I thank Papa God for sending His angel. My sleep was sweet just as He promised.

Memories of the retreat come to the surface often. Occasionally a lady who witnessed the weekend will contact me and reflect on that time of over 40 years ago.

God has used his angelic host from the beginning and continues to use them for His purposes. God changes not. He is the same yesterday, today, and forever.

"For He will command His angels concerning you to guard you in all your ways"
(Psalm 91:11 ESV).

Points to Ponder

- Thinking back, have you ever experienced something similar in your own life?

- If so, what? Take time to journal about it, including emotions, positive or negative thoughts, questions you may have had.

Prayer

Our Loving Jesus, embrace me with Your faithfulness, Your constant safety, everlasting security and ceaseless protection.

ENCOUNTER

It's Not Over

I'm cleaning the floors, a task I'm not particularly fond of. My mind is void of any particular thoughts or concerns. I hear an audible voice saying, "It's not over!"

What? What's not over? Of course, it's not over. Our company is coming and I have lots of floors yet to clean.

Then, I hear the angelic realm echo "NO! It's not over." Okay, so I realize this is a message the angels are bringing from Papa God. They gently tell me to write down my thoughts and I will find understanding to share.

Have you been feeling you are not accomplishing what Papa God wants you to do? Do you find your vision has waned? Have your dreams diminished? Are you feeling discouraged or dejected?

The heavenly messenger voices call out "You are not neglected!"

God laughs at the enemy, it's true, He does, as the enemy tries to cause defeat in our lives.

You are His temple. You are a source of the supply of God. Because of the Cross, you experience the person-hood of God and are filled with His Glory. You execute His message of the justice of God, which is True Love, from the position of the loving relationship that you have with Him and He has with you.

Papa God wants you to know that His plan has never been that the older or more experienced beloved ones should "move to the back of the church." Our culture says we get to a certain age and we have to move to the back. Church culture seems to dictate that our purpose when we reach a certain age is basically to support the young ones who are receiving the revelations. Papa says that is NOT His plan!

Older people are marginalized by our culture, by society, but not by God. Less experienced Christians are often marginalized by the church culture, but not by God. God is not exclusively age oriented. God is not exclusively experience oriented. He wants all of His body working together; working side by side; encouraging one another. He longs to have the older generation encourage the younger; the younger encourage the older; the experienced encourage and validate the less experienced; the beginners encourage the experienced ones to keep on seeking, finding, and sharing.

No one, and no words are allowed by God to rob you of the hunger you have for Him, and the hunger He has for you to be together with Him.

"He is causing all of us to be in the motion of Holy Spirit's moving in the frequencies of heaven!" Can you hear the angels gathering? They are waiting for God to call His heavenly messengers to do God's bidding when He hears the decrees and declarations of His heart being lifted up by us, His family.

God has a plan and a purpose, and you get to continuously fellowship with that plan and purpose.

Do you ever hear yourself telling Papa God "I can't do that! It's too hard" when you know He has something for you to accomplish? He replies "Are you kidding Me? I live in you and I can do all things!" Jesus does not want you separate from Him. He does not want what you do to be a "here's your thing" and then what He is doing to be a "here's My thing."

Let Him show you more things from His heart, and infuse you with encouragement, strength, confidence and identity. He wants to impart revelations and understanding of the mysteries and scrolls that He has long ago deposited within your spirit.

You have His divine nature within you. You are qualified as world changers! No matter what your experience has been, no matter what your age, rise up and occupy your space in the Spirit. Receive far beyond what your heart has been crying out for. It is not over!

Tap into God's abundance, God's prosperity. You are the one to discover! You are His mouth piece, you are His signpost. His message through you creates reality. It comes from God's Throne overflowing with grace and mercy.

I hear the angels in one accord again proclaiming the word of God "it's not over for any of you!" There is so much more than we can think or imagine in Jesus.

What an awesome, amazing break from cleaning floors! I'll share it all, Lord! You've sent Your messengers on an assignment for me to meditate deeply on Your constant loving regard for us and all that we bring to the advancement of the Kingdom of God.

"Since my youth, God, You have taught me, and to this day I declare Your marvelous deeds"
(Psalm 71:17 NIV).

Points to Ponder

- What would it look like for you to "occupy" your space in the Spirit today?
- Define your understanding of the word occupy.
- How has God uniquely equipped you to minister in and to the Body of Christ at the age and place where you are right now?

Prayer

God Almighty, I call out to you wondering if there is more. Assure me You have an anointed place that only I can fill in the Kingdom of God.

SMALL SIGHTINGS

Lemur Angel

After a Bible study I was sitting in the front seat of my vehicle with a friend, discussing the desires in our hearts to be able to do what we feel the Lord is calling us to do. We don't have a direction to follow at this time however. So, we pray and ask the Lord for guidance, knowledge, and wisdom. It is evening and the sky is getting dark. About a block away I see what appears to be an airport Marshall, his large red batons in his hands standing in the middle of a street directing cars. I share what I am seeing. My friend sees him also. Together we watch as he lifts his batons straight up, to the left, and to the right. It is a curious thing to observe. He seems so out of place in a neighborhood rather than on an airport tarmac.

I jump back, my heart pounding, when suddenly the "Marshall angel" is on the hood of my car, looking straight into my front window. His eyes are disproportionately huge! My friend is startled also. We are perplexed at why he is looking at us. What is he telling us? Why was he directing traffic a block away?

Then we laugh together. God has sent an angel to show that He directs our ways. We can rest in the confidence that He will guide us in the new paths we are to walk in and in the awesome spiritual adventures He has designed for us.

"The LORD says, 'I will guide you along the best pathway for your life. I will advise you and watch over you"
(Psalm 32:8 NLT).

We refer to this angelic being as the "lemur angel". His wide-opened round eyes remind us of the primate lemur.

Points to Ponder

- Is there a mentor, pastor, friend who reminds you that God directs our ways and guides us in the awesome adventures He has for us?
- Do you need that reminder often? Why or why not?

Prayer

God, I know, I can rest in the confidence that You will guide and direct me in the new paths I am to walk in. I am ready to engage in the awesome spiritual adventures You have designed for me.

ENCOUNTER

The Office Tower

"Good morning, ma'am." The doorman greets me kindly as he reaches for an impressive golden handle and slowly opens the large stately door. I smile, thank him, and step into the grand, luxurious Park Avenue style foyer of the office tower.

What a workplace wonder! I have to pause for a moment and observe the stunning flower arrangements, in cohesive color schemes, perfectly placed on tall marble tables.

Headed in the direction that most people are going, I stop at the elevators and wait expectantly for one of the doors to open. A few people exit the elevator allowing as many of us as possible to rapidly press into the confined space. Floor numbers are lit up as the elevator begins to climb. Designated floors have been reached and only a few of us are left inside as we reach the top floor. As I am exiting, I notice the office number directory signs. Pointing to the left is 4001-4015 and to the right is 4016-4031. I am on the fortieth floor, not knowing which direction I am to turn.

Approaching me is a distinguished looking gentleman in a tailored black suit. I can't place where I have seen him before, but it is nice to recognize a familiar face. "Good morning, sir. I know we have met, but I am very sorry I don't recall your name."

"Good morning." His reply comes with professionalism. "My name is Zavad. I know you well. Please walk with me to your office."

My office? Do I have an office on the fortieth floor of a building I have never been in before?

As I follow him my mind begins to reflect on possible meeting times with Zavad. He unlocks an office door and beckons me to enter before him. I'm drawn to the sight of a brilliant blue sky and snow-capped mountain peaks outside the massive walls of windows. Moving close to the windows I notice there are no buildings in sight. Only the green lush gardens below, trees reaching skyward, and the iridescent sparkle of a large river shimmering with movement is the spectacular beauty I see.

Zavad extends his hand, asking me if there is anything he can get for me. His body language indicates he is committed to helping and serving me. "May I have something to drink, please? And tell me, what am I to do here?" He smiles, opens double oak-paneled doors, and pulls out a gold cart with china plates, a lovely tea set, a colorful basket of fresh fruits, a loaf of delicious smelling fresh-baked bread, and a decanter of wine.

Puzzled as to where I am and why I am here, I place a few strawberries on a plate and sit in a comfortable chaise. Zavad sits in an adjacent high-back chair. Glancing around to my right, I see a large bookshelf, displaying a significant collection of various sized reading materials. It is a temptation for me to walk over and check out the possible storehouse of knowledge, but I hear Holy Spirit tell me that my purpose today is to *"come up here..."* Revelation 4:1, and to write down what I see and hear. I feel a sense of immense expectation for what is about to take place.

Holy Spirit is tangibly here with me. An awesome peace penetrates the atmosphere in this room. I think of *"The world cannot accept him, because it neither sees him nor knows him. But you know him for he lives with you and will be in you"* (John 14:17 NIV).

I'm contemplating how I came to this office. I remember getting dressed in the morning to head to the store and buy some groceries. Zavad said he knows me well. I believe Papa God uses angels to cause detours or circumstances in our lives to get us where Papa God is calling us. I'm now convinced that God's angel, Zavad has supernaturally taken me on detours in my life and this is again what is happening now.

Zavad walks over to a wall with large theater-type curtains covering it. He opens the curtains to reveal a scene from Old Testament times. I am physically set into the scene and watch in awe as I am close and can see Leah, Judah's mother, crying out and naming her fourth son Judah which means Praise.

The scene switches before me. Judah is now a grown man. He is standing with his 11 brothers before his father Jacob. Jacob tells the brothers to gather around so he can explain what will happen in days to come. Holy Spirit reminds me that what Jacob is about to declare is not for the Old Testament times, but rather for the last days which began when

Jesus was resurrected. I watch, seeing the spirit of prophecy coming on Jacob. He lays hands on each of his sons. When he gets to Judah, the tribe from which Jesus is going to come into the earth, he tells of the eternal symbols given to the New Covenant Church, the Tribe of Judah.

Holy Spirit reveals that Jacob, by the Spirit of God, is carried into the future to see the Lion of Judah opening the scroll. Jacob could never have seen this in the Old Covenant. It's all about Jesus, the Lion of the Tribe of Judah, the New Covenant given by Grace! My spirit is fluttering with excitement and jubilation!

I'm being shown an incredible passage right out of Genesis 49. I watch and see Jacob prophesying our Lord Jesus as the Lion, the Vine, the Scepter, the Ruler's Staff. He prophesies Jesus on the donkey, His Robe, His Blood, His Victory. What an experience to be right here, feeling the words of truth being set into the atmosphere as he speaks.

I think about times when many of us desire to hear a personal word from God. We often long to have someone speak to us on behalf of our Papa God. But we, as New Covenant believers and as the Tribe of Judah, have already been prophesied over. How overwhelming is that? That which Jacob prophesied then, would manifest in the New Covenant Church, after the Day of Pentecost. We are living in that time of prophecy fulfilled. Glory!

"Judah, your brothers shall praise you. Your hand shall be on the necks of your enemies; your father's sons shall bow down to you. Judah is a young lion—my son, you return from the prey. Like a lion he crouches and lies down; like a lioness who dares to rouse him? The scepter will not depart from Judah, nor the staff from between his feet, until Shiloh comes and the allegiance of the nations is his. He ties his donkey to the vine, his colt to the choicest branch. He washes his garments in wine, his robes in the blood of grapes. His eyes are darker than wine, and his teeth are whiter than milk"

(Genesis 49:8-12 BSB).

Zavad recognizes the expression of awe on my face and closes the curtain. I have just been escorted back with Jesus to an extraordinary time.

I thank Papa God for an amazing angelic detour this morning. Walking over to the cart, I pick up a glass of wine and a piece of bread. I commune with my Jesus, thanking Him for the New Covenant that was established with His shed blood. I thank Jesus that the New Covenant is not one of law, but one of amazing grace. I thank Him that we received the eternal symbols of redemption, reconciliation, justification and our being united with Him that were given to the New Covenant Church, the Tribe of Judah, just as Jacob prophesied.

Zavad gives me a nod of friendship, approaches the door, and leaves. What a morning to have been taken by God's angel to a high place with Jesus where the gardens exude peace, the trees are reaching upwards in praise, the river sings as it flows continuously, the sky is revealing His faithfulness, and the mountains resound in singing.

I'm home again, but buying groceries can wait. This is a time of reflecting on the goodness of Papa God, the love of Jesus and the indwelling of Holy Spirit.

A postscript: I look up the name Zavad. It's Hebrew and means 'Present'.

"I will sing of the goodness and lovingkindness of the Lord forever; with my mouth I will make known Your faithfulness from generation to generation" (Psalm 89:11 AMP).

Points to Ponder

- Take some time and visualize/imagine yourself in this high place with Jesus 'where the gardens exude peace, the trees are reaching upwards in praise, the river sings as it flows continuously, the sky is revealing His faithfulness, and the mountains resound in singing.'
- Then journal about what you see, experience, and feel.
- Consider the fact that Papa God values relationship with each one of us so much that He would plan such an extravagant experience in order to be known more intimately by you!

Prayer

Jesus, may Your revitalizing beauty surround and refresh me and may Your pleasing smile rest upon me. May I know You as the Lion of Judah!

ENCOUNTER

I'm The King Of The World

Driving with traffic on a five-lane freeway is an odd situation to be in when an angel briefly appears.

Not only is the angel visible before me, but he is lying on the hood of our vehicle, his head at the front, and his arms out to his sides. I am stunned, but curious, and ask out loud "what are you doing there? I am driving 70 mph! Fortunately, I am able to see through you!"

His position reminds me of Jack, the character in the movie Titanic, who was at the front of the Titanic with his arms straight up to shout and catch the wind as the ship sped through the waters.

"I'm the king of the world" shouts the angel excitedly just as the character Jack did in the movie. I have to almost laugh. This moment is captivating, amusing, and glorious all at the same time. Our God can use any avenue He chooses to speak to us. He gets our attention through His marvelous, creative ways.

"But Jesus Christ is the King of the world!" I emphatically emphasize Jesus Christ as I say this out loud. "Father is showing you the position of believers together in unity with Him" Holy Spirit speaks.

I contemplate the message as I continue to drive. I am quite sure Holy Spirit will remind me of seeing the 'angelic hood ornament' that He cleverly used to emphasize our kingly reign in this world. He desires it to permanently resonate in our minds and spirits until we live securely, confidently, and constantly in His power and authority that He has established in us.

Step into living life abundantly in power, dominion, and authority. JESUS and YOU are the king of the world!

"And hath made us kings and priests unto God and his Father; to Him be glory and dominion for ever and ever. Amen.

(Revelation 1:6 KJV).

Deeper Revelation

A reign (noun) is a period during which something or someone is dominant or powerful. To reign (verb) means to have kingly rule. Because of the authority of the word of God, we are destined to reign in life as a king and have God's power and dominion over all situations and provocations. In a country or nation with a kingdom, a reign is set to last the remainder of a monarch's life. No time limit.

Isn't it just like Papa God to once again illustrate our life in Him by showing the natural first through the angel positioning himself as Jack, the character in the Titanic movie who was declaring he is the king of the world? Then we see the spiritual aspect that we indeed are, as sanctified believers in Jesus Christ, ruling as kings and priests.

"The spiritual did not come first, but the natural and after that the spiritual" (1 Corinthians 15:46 NIV).

Jesus's power and authority has been given to us, as sons and daughters of our Most High God, to reign as kings and on the earth. This is who we are, where we live, with the power to exercise God's authority. We as New Testament kings and priests will rebuild, restore and renew the devastated places (see Isaiah 61:3,4,6 NIV).

Points to Ponder

- As priests we are able to present ourselves and represent others to God. Name some ways you are able to represent or lift someone before God. How do you present yourself to Him? As kings we have authority because of our posistion in Christ to represent God on earth. What attributes or characteristics of God do people see in you?
- What thoughts come to your mind as you read the scripture in Revelation 1:6?

Prayer

Papa God, help me to daily posture myself before You in worship and adoration as my King. Holy Spirit, reveal to me how I can step into living my life abundantly in the power, dominion and authority given to me by You.

ENCOUNTER

My Bible

I walked to the center of the platform and set my Bible down on the pulpit in preparation to speak at a conference. The first session had been intense and the atmosphere was extremely heavy. I was not aware as I stood there, but apparently Papa God wanted to exchange the heaviness with laughter.

As I greeted the people and began to share a message, my Bible and all of the papers tucked inside went flying off the pulpit onto the podium and the floor beneath. I was visibly startled! Pages of my favorite Bible and all my important pieces of paper with scribbled notes on them were strewn everywhere.

Holy Spirit whispered to me "the angels did this." I looked at the untidy mess on the floor and podium and answered Holy Spirit. "Really?" What a curious question to ask Holy Spirit who speaks only truth. I needed to share those words from Him with the bewildered audience. A few giggles were heard but attempts to suppress them increased in strength. One helpful person scurried to gather up the scattered pages and papers, and hand me my Bible. I held up the Bible for everyone to see and commented that it had been in an angelic windstorm and was close to complete disrepair. More giggles. As I opened my Bible to gain my composure and find a specific passage, I realized the entire New Testament was now in the front of my trusted Bible, and the complete Old Testament now in the back. This was just too crazy to not tell everyone what had happened. Very carefully holding up the Bible again, showing them the tattered pages, these words came flying out of my mouth. "Well, that's the way it should be! The New Testament is now in the front and the Old Testament is now in the back." Uproarious laughter hit us all. "We are living in the New Covenant." Cheers, applause and uninhibited laughter moved throughout the guests. The more we all tried to be composed, the more hysterical we became. "It's hard to stand up straight," I told them as my knees kept buckling. "Nobody fall asleep, I may need you up here to preach." Previously solemn people became unrestrained and animated. I was not able to address the group with my original message. Sporadic thoughts of needing to convey my intended message were silenced. Everything I said caused more hilarity.

God had taken over! There was no need for me to share a serious message. God was determined to captivate us all in joy and refreshment. Holy Spirit and the angels continued to turn the entire session into unrestrained, infectious laughter! Lunchtime carried a lot of volume that day. Humorous comments and giggles were shared across tables. The reality of trying to converse while recalling the incident without everyone's entire body reacting in gleeful delight was an added blessing from Papa God. There was no space for depression, anxiety, tension, stress or even unbelief. We needed the refreshing He brought to us through our contagious convulsing laughter. The atmosphere was so light that there were joy bubbles floating in it! God is amazingly good! His smiling face shone upon, beside and within us.

"Our mouths were filled with laughter and our tongues with shouts of joy"
(Psalm 126:2 NIV).

"This is the day that the Lord has made; let us rejoice and be glad in it"
(Psalm 118:24 ESV).

"Be glad in the Lord and rejoice, O righteous, and shout for joy all you upright in heart!"
(Psalm 32:11 ESV).

Points to Ponder

- When has laughter taken over any anxiety, depression, fear, or stress within you?
- Was it an intense overthrow?
- Did you feel like shouting for joy?

Prayer

Lord God, I ask for Your pure joy, the gladness of heart to fill me. Yours, oh God is the inward kind of joy. Bring it forth like a bubbling, gushing river in me.

Prayer Request & a Nursery Rhyme

A small group of us are praying. A prayer request is given for an individual who is extremely distressed because his family won't come to church. He had invited them to church, they joined him, but would not come back.

Two angels appear, sitting on the floor in front of us. They are singing and doing the hand motions to the nursery rhyme song "Pease porridge hot, Pease porridge cold. Pease porridge in the pot, nine days old." It is the song and clapping motions children used to sing so many years ago. The angels repeatedly continue singing this song for quite a while.

Some conversations are taking place among the people present, but the angels don't seem to mind. They appear confident in their ordained assignment from God. Without looking up at us, they keep clapping their hands with the motions of the song. "Pease porridge hot." The longer I observe them singing this song the more I know they are bringing a profound message. But what does "Pease porridge hot" mean? None of us seem to know. We continue to watch the angels with no concrete discernment of what they are conveying. Praying to God, we ask Him to clarify the meaning of this nursery rhyme the angels are illustrating.

Deeper Revelation

Late that night, after our time ended, I quickly looked up the song "Pease Porridge Hot." It originated in the 1700's in England when people, probably peasants, would have a big pot, put legumes in it and cook it for a meal. Then the next day they would add more to make it available again. If they left it for nine days and kept adding to what was left in the pot originally, it became contaminated.

This simple explanation led me to realize that most people like the teaching of what Jesus is doing and what He has done to be very hot, new, and fresh revelation. Others will leave it a day or so, adding more to the teaching that they believe is further revelation. But then there are those who add so much extra from all different sources that the revelation is tainted, not fresh, not pure, and doesn't satisfy or feed their spirit. When it gets contaminated a fresh start with a new, clean pot is necessary.

No, "Pease porridge hot" was not of this world. Father God was using the angels to give a message to the concerned gentleman. His family needed a fresh word. Not old and decaying. My friend delivered this unusual word, telling the man of the angels singing and clapping to "Pease porridge hot" and the interpretation Holy Spirit gave. She said his entire countenance changed as He heard this from the Lord. Recognizing that this was God speaking, peace washed over him! He believed God and prayed that he and his family would hear an uncontaminated message of the love of Jesus for them.

"Do not be conformed to this world, but be transformed by the renewal of your mind, that by testing you may discern what is the will of God, what is good and acceptable and perfect"
(Romans 12:2 ESV).

"And to be renewed in the spirit of your minds"
(Ephesians 4:23 ESV).

Points to Ponder

- Are there songs you have heard or games you have played that have a spiritual message to them? Identify any positive or nega tive messages and describe.

- Ask God to speak a fresh new message to you today from the Throne Room of God. Make sure to journal/record what He shows and speaks to you.

Prayer

Papa God, I ask that You speak a fresh, new message to me today. A message not just for me but one that I can share with others also, to bless them as well.

ENCOUNTER

Gold Bricks

A conference gathering of believers is about to convene. Outside the building people are standing in long lines, chatting among themselves to pass the time, anxiously waiting for doors to be opened. "I have read about this conference" one says to another. "I am wondering what it will be like." "Pretty soon we'll find out" a responder encourages.

Around the corner and out of the way of the crowd I see massive heaps of shining gold. These heaps surely are misplaced. But I see angels filling and holding heavy shovels full of various-sized gold bricks. What an odd sight I comment to myself. The large mounds of gold seem to be treasure troves of unknown origin.

Watching the movement of numerous angels shoveling gold bricks astonishes me. Soon they are entering the foyer of the building we are to occupy and completely covering the floors of our gathering rooms with gold bricks.

Those attending have been patiently awaiting the invitation to enter the building. Three large doors open and the people begin to walk in, but stop suddenly. Looking down at the floor they see the ominous gold bricks laying at their feet. Unsure and hesitant to walk on the bricks, the stream of people entering has stopped. Many call out "That's impossible." "It's going to hurt." "I can't walk on gold!" "What is this?"

One inquisitive, brave person steps forward, onto the gold bricks and is pleasantly surprised that it doesn't injure his foot. As he steps on more bricks of gold, they flatten out and liquid gold shoots out of each one. People scream with excitement and rush in the doors to step on the gold bricks.

Soon the place is filled to maximum capacity with people and gold alike. The entire floor is a deep pool of liquid gold, four to five feet deep. Christian brothers and sisters are wading in the gold. Many are immersing themselves fully in silky liquid gold! Laughter, shouts, cheers, voices full of discovery and wonder calling to one another have taken over the atmosphere. Childlike playing in the pure brilliance of gold has brought an amazing bond among the people, along with an aura of freshness and vibrancy. Many pick up handfuls of gold and pour it on their heads as well as the heads of anyone near them. The exhilaration of knowing Jesus is a reality.

This is not over. I can feel the angels behind me watching and clapping joyfully in enthusiastic praise and approval.

God, You are magnificent! You are such a giver of life! Indeed, *"every good and perfect gift is from above, coming down from the Father of heavenly lights, who does not change like shifting sand"* (James 1:17 NIV).

The joy of Jesus is so deeply rooted and God-inspired. Why would we desire anything else but You?

I wanted to inquire of an angel why the gold is in bricks, and why when people step on them it causes the gold to become liquid.

Holy Spirit questions me, asking if I am aware when energy is added to a solid metal, the metal will melt. I had experienced it in a class years ago, understanding that particles break down because the particles in solids are rigid. When heat is applied the particles are loosened and start moving freely.

"God's Presence within you becomes that energy that causes the gold to melt." Holy Spirit explains. "His floodgates of blessings then open and His unrestrained liquid gold bursts out as streams from the Throne of God."

Holy Spirit continues "as you set aside any hesitancy and move out with confidence into more of the available unknown of God and His Kingdom realm, old beliefs, bondages and strongholds are broken. You walk into your true, pure, authentic path with Him. You are joined in His power and authority. We want all who are here to experience first-hand the intense melting power of bondages and strongholds."

Conference participants have become euphoric playing in the gift of His gold. I am quite sure this was not the norm of past experiences with this particular conference, but God chose to bless us and speak to us in His unique way. I continue to observe angels bringing in more shovels full of gold bricks, depositing them on the floor. They watch with satisfaction as the gold bricks become liquid and people are gleefully set free from rigid bondages and strongholds in His Presence.

The gold of His Throne, His Son Jesus, His word, His love, His power and His authority is our treasure trove.

"Yes, the Almighty will be your gold and your precious silver; for then you will have your delight in the Almighty, and lift up your face to God"
(Job 22:25-26 NKJV).

"...you are like the wings of a dove covered with silver and its pinions glistening gold"
(Psalm 68:13b NASV).

"By your wisdom and understanding, you have acquired riches for yourself and have acquired gold and silver for your treasuries"
(Ezekiel 28:4 NASB).

Points to Ponder

- Has God's pure love as gold ever flooded over you, engulfed you?
- What does it mean that Almighty God will be your gold and your precious silver? Is He your invaluable treasure of joy, freedom and completeness?
- Have you had a similar encounter? If so, journal your experience.

Prayer

Lord God, thank You that Yours is an unfathomable, everlasting, relentless love that You lavish on me as Your cherished one. May Your unconditional love be as liquid gold being poured out.

ENCOUNTER

Sapphires

After a day of meetings, I'm relaxing in a chair with my feet up. A conversation with Jesus brings joy and refreshing to my body and spirit.

My eyes catch sparks of flashing brilliant blue lights coming from the hallway toward our front door. Is a storm brewing? Is there lightning outside? I start to get up out of my chair, but the vivid light approaches me at amazing speed and hovers above my right foot. There is no opportunity to study what has happened as a second blue light appears and settles above my left foot.

Knowing these are angels on assignment from the Throne Room, I hear an announcement in heavenly voices that all of heaven apprehends. "Behold the ankles of the Bride of Christ!" What an unusual declaration. Ankles?

I'm aware that angelic activity is increasing exponentially. I anticipate having angelic encounters often, and gratefully receive the company of angels. But sometimes, accompanying explanations are extremely helpful to fully understand the meaning of the message the angel brings.

My eyes are closed, contemplating that very peculiar declaration. I feel a slight weight on my feet and sense objects are being placed around my ankles. It is an odd sensation. I look and see shimmering blue sapphire stones encircling each of my ankles. What is the purpose of these beautiful gemstones?

Holy Spirit knows my question and lovingly responds. He explains that an ankle is made up of three bones. These bones together work as one to support each person's weight to enable each to stand on their feet.

"We are Triune God, three working together as one supporting the Body of Christ, allowing her to stand. The sapphires placed upon you are your authority, calling you to deeper revelations of *I AM* and who you are in us. They pull you outward and upward, to the majesty of

Father, to new beginnings, and to new encounters with us. Behold your ankles. Recognize the authority, integrity, loyalty, freedom, and justice you stand and move in. The Throne of Grace and your sapphire gems are forever with you."

I'm in awe of the sight of the gems around my ankles. Thank you, Papa God for sending angels with an extraordinary message reminding me of the complete power and authority received from You. Thank You that You remind us we forever walk in freedom to co-labor with Christ. Our sapphires are permanently placed. We are standing firm. Sapphires from heaven for the Body of Christ. What awesome divine love.

"Then they climbed the mountain—Moses and Aaron, Nadab and Abihu, and seventy of the elders of Israel—and saw the God of Israel. He was standing on a pavement of something like sapphires—pure, clear sky-blue"
(Exodus 24:9-10 Message).

"And above the firmament that was over their heads was the likeness of a throne, as the appearance of a sapphire stone, and upon the likeness of the throne was the likeness as the appearance of a man above upon it"
(Ezekiel 1:26 KJV).

Points to Ponder

- Do you stand firm in your understanding of His authority and power within you? Why or why not?

- Do you sense how Triune God functions in harmony, and that the Three-in-One together continuously support you?

- Why do you think God had His angels bring sapphires as His choice to represent power and authority?

Prayer

Father God, thank You for reminding me that I forever walk in freedom to co-labor with Christ. Allow me to receive and understand the deeper revelations of *I AM* and who I am in You. I'm ready to receive new encounters and new beginnings with You!

SMALL SIGHTINGS

Cotton Candy

I was feeling renewed and rejuvenated. This was the end of the fabulous conference I had just attended. A friend joined me as I was standing outside waiting for my ride to the airport. We began visiting and sharing thoughts about the awesome conference we were so blessed to have been a part of.

Unexpectedly an overwhelming feeling of bewilderment came upon both of us. We instantly looked at each other and simultaneously asked "do you smell cotton candy?" Yes, absolutely. We were perplexed at having our noses tickled by the unusual aroma, but agreed. Each of us had a vivid awareness of the unique smell of cotton candy. We had no other description available for this permeating scent. Cotton candy was definitely what we were encountering. We questioned a passerby if he smelled it. "Smell what? Cotton candy?" he asked. "No." With a chuckle he shook his head and walked on. We asked another and still the answer was no. The scent of cotton candy ebbed and flowed but did not vanish. It came and went like a wave, strongly gripping our senses then lightly releasing them momentarily.

We continued to check our surroundings. No one was eating the candy. No one was selling it. Cotton candy was nowhere around. The strong aroma in our nostrils became intense. Our curiosity had not been satisfied. We continued to comment about the overwhelming scent of cotton candy which seemed to have overtaken the atmosphere.

Simultaneously we grasped the significance of this aroma and realized it was the presence of an angel! God was showing us we had all of our senses activated during the conference we had attended. A supernatural occurrence was happening again. The anointing of the conference was not over. An angel named Cotton Candy was visiting us. No one had ever mentioned the existence of a cotton candy angel to either of us, but together we shared our new discovery. The cotton candy angel had visited us that day and as we enjoyed a few more whiffs before my ride appeared, we knew there were more visitations to come from the Cotton Candy angel.

Soon after our encounter, my friend was a guest on a Christian podcast. She shared with me that in the studio she again recognized the smell of the cotton candy angel. She had mentioned it to the hostess and was told that yes, the cotton candy angel was there. The hostess is well known for encountering angels and stated that the cotton candy angel changes atmospheres, ministers joy, laughter, jubilation, and the lightening of any weights that have been carried. It was the confirmation we needed.

"Ointment and perfume rejoice the heart: so doth the sweetness of a man's friend by hearty counsel."
(Proverbs 27:9 KJV).

Points to Ponder

- Have you encountered aromas, fragrances, and odors that bring back vivid memories?

- When recalling any of these memories, did you interpret the symbolic symbolic meaning differently from the known description of the aromas, fragrances anand/odors? Explain.

- Have you noticed a change in the spiritual atmosphere or in your mental or emotional state in connection to aromas?

Prayer

Jesus, I pray for the experience of feeling and sensing the sweet-smelling fragrance of Your presence and anointing poured out upon me, Your favored one.

ENCOUNTER

Tapping

"What's on Your heart this morning, Papa God?" I ask while headed down the hall to the empty classroom I will occupy for a portion of the day. Passing a mom holding an infant, I smile at the baby, sweetly telling him good morning. He turns his sleepy head into his mamma's shoulder. She comments how bashful he is. "His confidence will come soon." We both laugh at the mental picture of what is possible for this little one.

My room is quiet. The familiar table and chair are beckoning me to sit and be still. "Papa, what is on Your heart?" As I ask and begin seeking Him, a light tap, tap, tap is coming from the window. No one is looking through the glass. I figure a bird may have landed on the ledge and started pecking at the glass. But then I hear it again and decide to move closer, focusing with curiosity on the windowpane.

As I do, a blue, obscure blurred form swiftly moves across the space of the window. I know it's an angel. This one is not as clearly defined to me as others have been, but the brilliance of the blue light is undeniable.

My first instinct is to go to the door and let him in. Before I can move, the blue light is settling at the table where I sit. I am sensing an ensuing conversation is at hand.

My spirit becomes alive with expectation. This is an appointed time. The silence is broken, and the sounds of heaven are distinctively audible in my room. Waves of the harmonies quietly roll into a melodic theme of a chamber orchestra and then crescendo like a grand philharmonic orchestra playing a rich symphonic poem. Taking in this glorious sound, I shut my eyes and feel the heavenly waves flowing over me. LOVE is here, and He has one of His messenger angels with Him!

The music decreases slightly. I hear the angel vigorously announce "Be bold! Be strong! For the Lord thy God is with you!"

I can't help it. This causes me to remember a song we sang in Sunday School. I burst into singing the chorus, "Be bold! (be bold) Be strong! (be strong) For the Lord… thy God is w-i-i-i-t-h you!" It makes me chuckle remembering how fun and upbeat the song was to sing years ago. We always made the word "with" last an extremely long time.

By declaring in song what the angel announced from the Throne Room, I am agreeing, placing the declaration of our boldness and strength into the atmosphere. In years past singing and enjoying the song was void of understanding the true power of our words. "Be Bold!" I declare into the airspace again. Two simple yet strong, effective words.

"What else does Papa God want to make known?" The angel's voice rises from within the blue light. "Tell the Body of Christ to take risks with fearlessness and confidence."

"Act innovatively" he continues. "Move forward without hesitation to introduce the powerful encounters and deeper revelations. *I AM* desires to write volumes on the tablets of your hearts and spirits. Encourage one another often in the midst of this culture of confusion."

"And you show that you are a letter from Christ delivered by us, written not with ink but with the Spirit of the living God, not on tablets of stone but on the tablets of human hearts"
(2 Corinthians 3:3 ESV).

"He proclaimed the kingdom of God and taught about the Lord Jesus Christ with all boldness and without hindrance"
(Acts 28:31 NIV).

Wanting to be able to study this angel and ask him his name, I clear my throat to speak. But the brilliant blue form that shared the heart of Papa God with me is nowhere to be seen. It was such a short visit. I would have preferred he stayed longer. The intensity I felt in the room while he was here has not diminished. The residue of his visit plus the tangible presence of love, along with the glorious songs of heaven, bring a stillness and serenity to my soul and spirit. I am in awe that Papa would order this brief encounter.

Dig Deeply, Receive Freely, Share Boldly.

Deeper Revelation

My prayer is that our eyes will see, and our spirits comprehend new strategies and avenues to share the depths of who God is, and who we are because of Jesus. Ignite Your fire of passion and boldness in our midst, Lord Jesus. We desire to be encouragers through our testimony and to witness atmospheric change within our sphere of influence. Let it be a ripple effect, spreading rapidly as the earth is filled with the knowledge of the Glory of the Lord.

Points to Ponder

- What does it mean for you to: Dig Deeply, Receive Freely, and Share Boldly?
- Do you struggle to move forward in the things of God without hesitation? If so, why do you think you struggle?
- How can you help to introduce others to the powerful encounters and deeper revelations of God?

Prayer

Papa God, I want to be bold and strong, and to take risks with fearlessness and confidence. Help me to move forward without hesitation to embrace the deep revelations and powerful encounters You have for me.

ENCOUNTER

Bread Lines Again?

Often even when I am in my kitchen, an angel takes me by the hand and causes us to be airborne. I am surprised as again in my kitchen I feel my hand being held and we travel together to a part of the city which is unfamiliar to me. Suddenly we are on top of a large cliff overlooking a long line of thousands of people. Eight across, twelve across, thousands of people. I am puzzled at what I see. I stare at the mass of people and the angel asks me. "What do you see?" I'm not sure if it is my spirit, or my carnal mind responding but I ask, "is this a question like the Lord asked Jeremiah?"

"The word of the Lord came to me. What do you see Jeremiah? I see the branch of an almond tree, I replied. He Lord said to me, "you have seen correctly, for I am watching to see that my word is fulfilled"
(Jeremiah 1:11-12 NIV).

Then in a moment we have arrived at a new city location, but seeing the same situation. "What do you see?" He questions me. I don't answer because instantly He lifts me up and we are suddenly hovering over another massive group of people in yet another city.

This continues for quite some time. We travel to so many urban areas, seeing the same sight. The angel and I do not stay only in the United States and North America. We continue on. He brings me to cliffs above cities to see the same sights in Europe, South America, Africa, the Middle East, Asia, then Central America. It's a whirlwind, but the angel takes me around the world, pointing out the same enormous types of gatherings of people. I am confused. I want to know why he has me take note of all these people.

We end up on a cliff overlooking an ocean. It is a very calming sight at first but viewing the ocean and hearing the thunder of the crashing waves causes me to think of the nations and groups of people we have seen. I'm not sure where we are, which ocean I am enjoying with this angel. It doesn't really matter. We are silent for some time. Then the angel asks me the same question again. "What did you see?"

I respond "I observed so many people lined up, waiting. What are they waiting for?" I feel foolish answering him in this way, but I continue "it almost appeared to be the depression era bread lines." He grins and then quizzes me "tell me what you know regarding bread lines."

"I recall the bread lines were common in the United States during the 1930's." He asks me why that particular time in history was called The Great Depression and what else I knew about the bread lines. "The money supply in the United States collapsed because of panic and an economic downturn in the industrialized world. Many unemployed people were desperate to survive. They stood in lines to receive free bread and nourishment being distributed by the government."

Unexpectedly two warm, gentle hands cover my eyes. I reach up to place my hands on them in an attempt to identify whose they are. "It's Jesus." the angel whispers. I want to hold His hands tightly, but they slip carefully from my eyes. Now I see with clear understanding and discernment what the angel is showing me.

I exclaim in a loud voice "Countless numbers of people in this world are desperate, homeless, depressed, and wanting to survive! Countless want to be healed and whole! It IS a Bread Line! They are in line for the Bread of Life, JESUS!"

Seeing the cities and areas where the angel has taken me is an indication of the multitudes, even in this day, who are waiting for a touch from Jesus, our Provider. Some have a new revelation of Him and are telling others there is LIFE in Jesus. He sustains us. He frees us from depression. He provides for the destitute. He is the Healer. He calls us to His Home. We are united with our Triune God.

Countless numbers have not heard the good news of Jesus but are seeking and have been told these lines that appear to me as 'bread lines' have the answer. In these lines people longing to hang on to hope, longing to hang on to a relationship which is unending have discovered the answer. God knows. God is love. God will never forget the needy.

My emotions react. I ask the angel his name. "Elyacaph." I inquire of Elyacaph "what can I do?" He smiles and says "you have seen. Pray for those you have seen to receive the True Bread which came down from heaven. Pray that you step out in the love of Jesus when you see people in the seeking lines. Introduce them to the One who loves them unconditionally, just as they are."

Elyacaph continues to instruct me. "Pray for the new additions to the family of God to be nurtured and nourished. Pray that the family of God supports each other, adds their strength to these new ones, and loves as God loves, I'm here to help."

Releasing a huge breath of joy, I'm observing the bread lines changing, becoming lengthy lines of delight and celebration intertwining from city to city, nation to nation, tribe to tribe. The family of God is uniting. There are no oceans or seas separating us. We are one with Jesus. We are holding each other, taking care of each other, loving each other. There is no condemnation. The family of God is rejoicing! This is what God is wanting!

The angel named Elyacaph pats my back and affirmingly says, "you have seen well." I am immediately back in my home, standing alone in my kitchen. I believe I was transported forward in time, having seen the transition which is currently taking place. The body of believers is growing, manifesting in wholeness and love.

Note: I later had to look up the spelling of Elyacaph's name, hoping I had heard and pronounced it correctly when he told me. It means "God increases the family."

My God will gather in those that seek Him!

"I am the living bread that came down from heaven. Whoever eats this bread will live forever. This bread is my flesh, which I will give for the life of the world"
(John 6:51 NIV).

"For the bread of God is he who comes down from heaven and gives life to the world"
(John 6:33 ESV).

"Jesus said to them, 'I am the bread of life. Whoever comes to me will never be hungry, and whoever believes in me will never be thirsty"
(John 6:35 ESV).

Points to Ponder

- Jesus is the bread that never perishes, never runs out, and never spoils. Ask God to help you step out in the love of Jesus when you see people in lines for the Bread of Life. Introduce them to the One who loves them unconditionally, just as they are.

- How do you see yourself helping to support others and loving the way God loves?

Prayer

Father God, allow me to be an active part of imparting the truth of who You are to the world around me. Allow me to speak and release the truth to those seeking, that Jesus is the bread of life, who is who He says He is, and who will do what He says He will do.

ENCOUNTER

Desert Ice Cream

A multi-colored ice cream stand with pictures of many flavors of ice cream painted around an open window is positioned close to me. It's a cheerful-looking little stand, welcoming those ready to be satisfied with delicious scoops of ice cream. The stand seems uniquely out of place, however. I am in the middle of a parched, barren desert region. The air temperature is extremely hot, and this vast area appears devoid of life. I am a few yards from the stand, sitting with my back against a pile of sand that must have been formed by a recent dust storm. No one is around. No one is at the stand asking for ice cream. It's extremely quiet. I'm wondering why I am here.

My attention is drawn to a man who comes into view inside the stand. He has a clean white apron on, is ready to serve, and is whistling a joyful tune. He seems to be expressing tremendous pleasure that he can provide a delightful respite from the scorching temperatures of the desert.

Three young children approach the front of the ice cream stand. The youngest looks to be about four, the middle one maybe six and the oldest is eight or nine years old. They are longingly looking over the list of available ice cream. The oldest one, a girl, checks her pockets and shrugs. I can tell they have no money to buy a refreshment. But the man inside the stand indicates he will give them ice cream cones even if they don't have money to pay. He smiles cheerfully at each child, causing their faces to beam huge smiles back at him. He takes their order for a cone. I see him scoop out two scoops of ice cream which he thoughtfully places within each cone. As he hands the children their cones he says "This will keep you cool in this heat. Today is a very good day. You will have such fun!" Then he gives the children a quick light-hearted see-you-soon wave with his hand and begins cleaning his work counter.

With that the two young girls and boy move away from the stand, enjoying their refreshing cold treats. They start to examine the ice cream cones in their hands, comparing cones and talking inquisitively. Focusing from a distance on their cones I spot two additional scoops of ice cream which have been added to each double scoop they already have. All three children suddenly notice me and come running towards me calling out "Grandma, why? How did this happen? Look at all the ice cream!" I don't know them, but I am thrilled by their use of the endearing term "Grandma" when addressing me.

We are all perplexed at what we see has happened. I have no concrete answer to give them. "I'm not sure why there are now four scoops of ice cream instead of two" I answer. "Maybe because the ice cream is melting, and you cannot eat it fast enough. Or could it be that the man in the ice cream stand understands how quickly the ice cream melts and he is giving you more?" They all have puzzled looks on their sweet faces when immediately the four scoops become ten. Ten scoops! This is amazing! How is it possible?

The children are now joyfully dancing and twirling with glee while holding ice cream cones. "It's real! It's real!" the oldest girl shouts! They have passed the state of being fascinated. They are completely accepting the multiplication they have just witnessed as a miracle. The atmosphere has become electrified with excitement!

Immediately I look up and see a ladder beside each child. There is nothing high to climb up to. There is no need for a ladder in the middle of a desert. Yet each child now is standing next to a ladder. The young boy is very adventurous. He climbs up the ladder and begins to eat his frozen treat as fast as he can, hoping it won't melt. "I like eating from the top" he comments. My grandma instinct kicks in, and I rush over to hold him and the ladder. He is unaware of any possible danger.

The two girls also climb up their ladders. All three children are now on the highest ladder rung eating cones that are excessively full of ice cream. I notice the treats are melting rapidly. On the ground under each ladder are puddles of melted ice cream.

Snakes, rodents, reptiles, even a desert tortoise slowly begin crawling and creeping towards us from all directions. They must sense there is available food. I am contemplating where they came from and how they came so quickly. The children look at the creatures from their ladders. They are not scared, nor bothered. Suddenly all three children start purposefully knocking off the scoops of ice cream, letting them fall to the ground.

More and more desert critters come crawling. The children get down off the ladders and hold out handfuls of ice cream so the creatures can eat. As each scoop of ice cream disappears another scoop shows up. The oldest girl says, "I hear the man in the ice cream stand telling me just say what you need". The children are so pure and accepting. They begin to call out "more ice cream, and water for them to drink." I can tell the three youngsters are getting much satisfaction out of seeing the creatures thriving now. Over and over as the three call out their needs, more ice cream and containers of water are visible. The desert animals eat and drink until they have saturated themselves. Three brave children gather the creatures up, checking each one to see that it has no injuries. There is an indescribable connection happening between the animals and the children.

Out of the corner of my eye I see the man from the ice cream stand approaching. He stands next to me bearing a huge smile on his face. He winks, addressing the children. "God's words spoken through you will do the same thing as I do. Your words can create." As he says this the children come running over to him. He gives them all a hug and lovingly says to them "I see how you started out wanting ice cream for yourself. It changed when you saw the need of the creatures. You called out what you needed and received more ice cream and water. You made sure the creatures were fed and taken care of." The three youngsters hug him back and squeal with delight "We are happy the animals are full. We want to be like you!"

My heart begins beating profusely. I recognize this has been Jesus all along. I can feel His heart pulsating with love. Every beat sends electrical waves of love into the air which we all see. I capture waves in my hands and give them to each of the children. The three young ones now begin to catch waves on their own. Waves of love, waves of glory are enveloping all of us. This is pure, unconditional love coming from Jesus' heart. Everywhere I look I see His love. The Presence of God is resting upon all of us.

Jesus tells the children He must go. Their voices quiver a bit as they say, "Don't go." He assures them He is always with them and will always talk with them, even if they can't see Him. Jesus takes each of the children into His arms, tenderly kisses their foreheads, and blesses His cherished little ones.

Before He leaves, He turns and speaks to me saying, "these children are precious to me. Help nurture their inborn sense of wonder and trust. Remind them that they have an unseen Heavenly Father and a best friend Jesus who watches over and cares for them. Help them find their security in My strong love. Tell them how I changed water into wine and how I multiplied loaves and fishes to feed so many." He adds "these young ones will not forget their experience of creating from their spoken word. Helping the creatures will soon become helping people and drawing them into My Kingdom. Let them know they are able to do what I did because I am in them. I placed the ladders as a gateway between heaven and earth. As they climbed the ladders, I was depositing revelation into them. The seeds of My words within them will grow and bring a harvest."

My heart is still racing listening to the One sharing His words with me. Gratefully I respond, "yes Jesus, I will lovingly nurture them in their walk with You." And with those words He ceases to be visible.

Glancing over where the ice cream stand once was, only a few small puddles of ice cream are still in the dirt. The ladders are gone also.

I hug each of the children knowing they represent my grandchildren as well as all children. I recognize the undeniable love of Jesus within each of them. I tell them I will see them again. They gleefully respond, "Okay Grandma!" and skip away. I watch these little ones disappear and put my hand on my heart. "Yes, Jesus. The desert ice cream taught me well. All of us are Your children, having all of You within us."

Yes, Jesus, the desert ice cream taught me well. All of us are your children, having all of You within us.

I heard the resounding declaration of God's heavenly messengers, "Hallelujah! Hallelujah!"

"And He took the children one by one in His arms and blessed them with kind, encouraging words placing His hands on them"
(Mark 10:16 AMP).

"But Jesus called the children to him and said 'Let the little children come to me, and do not hinder them, for the kingdom of God belongs to such as these"
(Luke 18:16 NIV).

Deeper Revelation

Ice cream in the desert was not only for the children to experience, but also for me. I believe that from the foundations of the earth we are created to recognize and respond to God's voice. These cherished children did just that. The innocence, excitement, and pure trust of the children, in addition to tangibly experiencing His perfect love and Presence emotionally moved me today.

Points to Ponder

- Jesus devoted time for children. He loves them, protects them, is gentle with them, and tells us *"unless you change and become like little children, you will never enter the Kingdom of heaven. Therefore, who ever humbles himself like this child is the greatest in the kingdom of heaven"* (Matthew 18:3-4 NIV).

- Tell how children's inquisitiveness and their simple, uncomplicated manner of receiving can affect your emotions.

- What thoughts come to you as you read Matthew 18:3-4 NIV?

Prayer

Lord God, I know how precious children are to You. Help me to nurture their inborn sense of wonder and trust. Allow me to sow seeds and impart the truth that You, Jesus, are their best friend who watches over and cares for them. I also ask that You would continue to deposit revelation in me and allow the seeds planted in my own life and theirs to grow and bring in a great harvest for the Kingdom of God.

ENCOUNTER

Her Water Jug

During the school year I stay at my granddaughter's preschool. They have graciously given me a room in their facility, so for four hours I am by myself in the room. Most days are spent with Jesus and Holy Spirit. What a glorious gift of time that is.

When having a quick conversation with Jesus, I speak from my heart and say "Are You able to use me where you need me? I'm willing."

There is an immediate response on His part and rapidly an angel transports me to a poverty-stricken rural part of a country. From the pictures I have seen and what I have read, I assume I am in the African continent.

The temperature is exceptionally hot and the oxygen poor environment causes me to have difficulty breathing. There is no vegetation in this area, and no vehicles. Stray dogs frantically scavenge for food, eating anything they can find. Men and women with loose fitting clothing wander aimlessly without a fixed direction. A few naked or scantly clothed children are kicking rocks on the dusty road while younger ones are carried by their mothers.

It appears to be a busy part of the town. I am walking among the people on the dirt road also, noticing my surroundings. My eye catches the sight of a woman sitting on the side of the road a good distance away from me. Everyone is ignoring her as if she doesn't exist. People are passing directly in front of her and paying no attention to her. She has on a long cotton skirt and a top with minimal coverage. I purposefully take note of her skirt because she is sitting in the dirt, one knee bent upwards with her skirt covering her legs.

She has a pottery water jug in front of her, between her legs. I know she is begging for help. The woman appears to be very disheartened and dejected knowing this is her way of life. Day after day she must have come to the same spot, hoping someone will notice and share a taste of water with her.

I begin approaching her. As I walked closer to her, she glances up at me. Her eyes tell me she is tired and worn. I am a newcomer, maybe she doesn't want me to notice her. But she then looks straight into my eyes with a slight look of astonishment in her own eyes. The angel with me says she now is seeing Jesus, not me! She may not know or identify Jesus, but I believe she is not seeing a strange woman, but rather her Provider coming toward her. From Him hope is being extended to her spirit.

Walking up to her side without saying a word, I reach out and lovingly put my hand on her head. Immediately I'm witnessing a miracle. Able to see inside her container, I notice water filling the jug from the base rather than from the opening at the top. I watch in amazement as the jug becomes completely full of clean water. Jesus is working through me to meet this woman's needs.

People suddenly start to gather around her, peering into the once empty jug in amazement. Many are calling out for others to come and share in the excitement. A few are celebrating. She is not an outsider any longer. She is a miracle-receiving child of God! The angel who transported me here tells me she will become the talk of the community for generations. With awe and thanksgiving at what has just happened for this woman the angel takes me back to the classroom at preschool.

"For I was hungry and you gave me food. I was thirsty and you gave me drink, a stranger and you welcomed me"
(Matthew 25:35 NASB).

"Do not neglect to do good and to share what you have, for such sacrifices are pleasing to God"
(Hebrews 13:16 ESV).

"In the same way, let your light shine before others, so that they may see your good works and give glory to your Father who is in heaven"
(Matthew 5:16 ESV).

"Do not withhold good from those to whom it is due when it is in your power to do it"
(Proverbs 3:27 ESV).

Points to Ponder

- Have you witnessed a lonely, disheartened person become transformed before your eyes? Explain and share your reaction and/or the reaction of others also.

- How can you position yourself to not only receive your own miracle from God, but participate in helping others receive theirs?

Prayer

I want to be a miracle-receiving and miracle-giving child of God! Father God, show me what I must do to position myself to receive from You. Allow me to partner with You to help others receive Your miracles.

SMALL SIGHTINGS

Swooping Angel

Suddenly from just above the corner where the loft wall upstairs meets the family room wall came an angel swooping down with his arm and hand back by his shoulder. He does not have the appearance of other angels I have seen. I can see his head, arms, and hands. The rest of his body is wrapped in a lightweight, gray colored fabric, which is closed under his feet so they aren't visible. This sack-type covering, forming a tube around the angel is unusual. My natural thinking causes me to assume he must have a streamlined body allowing for his fast flight.

As he swoops down, his hand, with fingers spread, deliberately and almost forcefully pushes on my side. It knocks me backwards. After becoming upright, I watch as he does the same to the other four people in the room. He ascends and descends, swooping over each of the four, pushing on the side of each a few times. Immediately all of us are in a posture of receiving what the Lord is bringing us through this angel. Suddenly coming to a standstill, he boldly declares "Activation!"

I feel a turning and filling within my spirit and notice the others are experiencing a phenomenon within themselves as well. We came together to worship and have our retreat with God and what an awesome supernatural time He is giving us.

We have a few questions to ask the angel but he is not visible to us now. He has delivered an announcement from God's holy Throne of Grace and has disappeared after completing his assignment. We joyously, thankfully praise God.

The first rays of sunlight lit up the room we have stayed in throughout the night. As I am enjoying the early morning sun and a cup of steaming coffee, I hear "so what do you think?" I sense an angel on my right side, behind my shoulder. "What do I think about what?" He answers "about the swooping angel."

"Well, he came and announced activation." "How did he declare it?" responds the angel. "It physically felt somewhat forceful and very deliberate as if the angel was igniting a fire within me." I feel all these questions are to cause the four of us to realize this was a powerful awakening given by the swooping angel.

"*I AM* is revealing what has already been imparted and is now activated in you." Holy Spirit type shivers run up my spine as he continues to explain. "It is the dunamis power of *I AM* that is within each of you, but you have not been operating in it. Now it is fully functioning in and through you. You assuredly will be having opportunities to partake of His dunamis power, the same power that raised Christ from the dead, operating in you."

Deeper Revelation

The activation that the authorized angel announced was of the power, authority, grace and love of God that we already have within us. At times we need to be fully aware of, reminded of, and stirred up to use all that God has given us for the work of His Kingdom.

I look up the spiritual meaning of the color of his fabric covering. Gray indicates wisdom.

"And we impart this in words not taught by human wisdom but taught by the Spirit, interpreting spiritual truths to those who are spiritual"
(1 Corinthians 2:13 ESV).

"But the wisdom that comes from heaven is first of all pure, then peace-loving, considerate, submissive, full of mercy and good fruit, impartial and sincere"
(James 3:17 NIV).

Points to Ponder

- Have you received an impartation and/or activation from the Lord? If so, write down what you received and how you received it.
- Has this laid a foundation for what He has you doing?

Prayer

Papa God, I posture myself today to receive an impartation from You. I desire an impartation and activation of Your power, authority, grace and love within me to be used for Your divine purposes.

ENCOUNTER

The Tent of Meeting

In a quiet time with the Lord, I tell Him I know I am ready and ask Him if He will be willing to send me where He wants me to be.

Immediately an angel escorts me out of my chair, up into the air, and transports me to the inside of a large tent-like structure where a chief and others are sitting around a fire. I can smell the fire. Sparks are flying from the fire, but the tent is so large that the sparks dissipate before reaching the top of the tent. I appear to be in an African village. As I noticed my surroundings the Congo comes to mind. Dark skinned men around the fire must all be part of some kind of tribe.

The chief gestures for me to sit in the circle with them. I am given a fan which is the same as the men have. They are fanning the flame in unison, and I join in. The fan is the shape of a rowboat oar. It is the consistency of light balsa wood.

We sit and fan the flame together, up and down in a synchronized beat. This gives me an opportunity to study this tribe more closely. Each man is wearing a necklace full of chains and stones. All the men sit crossed-leg position, concentrating on the fire.

It seems that I have just arrived here, but I know it is time for me to leave already. The heavenly messenger raises me into the air and back to my chair in my room.

One week later I sense myself leaving and am taken back inside the same tent. I hadn't asked the Lord about going back. I was not expecting it.

When I arrive, the same chief and the other men were still sitting around the fire. Feelings of having just been there and leaving only momentarily confuse me. The men nod and acknowledge me, but I remain standing. I spot the intriguing necklaces again, beginning to study each one. My inquisitive studying stops as the one man I understand to be the chief slips his necklace over his head. As he does so, the necklace becomes pop beads. How surprisingly odd. He takes three of the pop beads, snaps them together and passes the three around the circle to the other men.

I watch the white, opaque beads being passed. Each man reaches for his own necklace which also becomes a strand of pop beads. This must be a very contrived ritual. Each man then adds a bead to the chief's original three. After each had added his bead, the chief hands me nine beads total to hold. Three from the chief and one from each of the six men. I don't have enough beads to make a necklace, but I need to hang on to them. Without the chief explaining, I understand the symbolism of when someone may receive a bead from me, then desire to give a bead away, more will be added to them. This must be an example of the fulfillment of scripture *"Give and it will be given to you. A good measure, pressed down, shaken together, and running over will be poured into your lap"* (Luke 6:38 BSB).

Is this visit over? I feel myself moving swiftly through the air and I am back in my room.

It is about seven months later. I am aware that Holy Spirit is going to take me back a third time. I am sitting in my chair, but now swiftly moving through the air and in the blink of an eye I walk through the open doorway of the same tent. All is the same. Time must have stood still.

The chief can communicate with me without speaking. He seems to perceive what I am thinking. I am able to understand him just by being near him. With his eyes he questions me about the beads I received from him. Slightly shaking my head to let him know I do not have the pop beads with me I watch as he takes his necklace off and sends it flying! As he flings it, it becomes only one bead which travels through the wall of the tent, to the outside.

I know I have to go out and find it. It had landed in front of a woman standing a good distance from the tent. She is cradling a baby whose head is hanging down over the edge of her arm. No gurgling or cooing is coming from the child. With a sickening feeling inside of me I realize the baby is lifeless. Compassion rises in my heart. I approach her, seeing her eyes full of tears. She is desperate, the longing of her aching heart for this baby that she birthed to live is heartbreaking. Pointing to the tent I motion to her to take the baby to the tent. She shakes her head as if to say emphatically "No! No! I can't!" There is such fear within her when she silently cries out.

Without hesitation I take the baby from her, enter the tent, and ask in my spirit if the chief would pray or somehow bring this baby back to life. He takes his necklace off. Instinctively I bend my head down as he places it around my neck. It is his FULL necklace. The pop beads have been replaced. He is telling me "YOU do it!! YOU have MY authority." Immediately after receiving his necklace, I understand clearly what he is telling me.

Baby sounds! I hear precious baby squeals. I haven't spoken a word or a command to the baby, resurrection life just happened when the tribal chief put his necklace on me.

Excitedly I reunite the baby with his joyful mother.

Back in the tent again I communicate my question to him. "Why am I the only female in here?" He crosses his arms over his chest indicating the sign for love. I know that sign! The chief is telling me to let people know ALL are welcome.

Now here I am, sitting back in my chair in my room. My unique trip to the tribe is over. There is so much to remember.

"But he said to me, 'My grace is sufficient for you, for my power is made perfect in weakness.' Therefore I will boast all the more gladly of my weaknesses, so that the power of Christ may rest upon me"
(2 Corinthians 12:9 ESV).

Deeper Revelation

I've contemplated these three amazing visits. Through prayer and investigating resource materials, I have had lots of questions answered. These experiences are difficult to explain by natural means. But I know that the supernatural, spiritual realm is the superior realm. These three encounters build on one another. Through them Holy Spirit is communicating in such an experiential way the love of the Triune God and the fullness I have in being His.

When we partake with God, wherever He takes us, whatever He shows us and uses, we receive a higher revelation of Him. We realize who we are in Him through experiencing and encountering Him, much more than we could grasp through our physical senses alone. All our senses are reacting to His life in us!

One strand perfectly formed by linking each bead to the others illustrates the bonding of believers united in the Father by His love.

When I returned for the second time, a week later in the natural, the tribe was in the same position, doing the same thing. No time had lapsed. The chief (Jesus) is continuously still doing what He has set out to do. He is still fanning the flame of God's power, stirring up the gifts of God within us.

The third and final time Holy Spirit took me there brought even more revelation.

The door of the chief's tent Is always open just as the door to Jesus is always open if we desire to enter. The woman was dealing with the lies she carried in her mind. Lies are the enemy's biggest and strongest weapon. She didn't need to fear, we are all free to call upon the Lord and come into His Presence.

I received ALL authority from the chief, who was Jesus. I didn't have to think about it, or analyze it. Healing just happened. And His Love directed me! This was a gospel encounter.

The necklace was weighty, as is His Glory. Even one little bead of His love, like the one the chief threw, can go through any walls we may have up, and break through any barrier.

As we walk in His light, His Kingdom shines through us. He will take us places where we will bring the truth that Jesus accomplished everything on the cross. It's all about Him, and Him in us! We co-labor with Him and bring that which is dead back to life!

"I will place on his shoulder the key to the house of David; what he opens no one can shut, and what he shuts no one can open"
(Isaiah 22:22 NIV).

Points to Ponder

- Do you know the door to the Lord's Tent of Meeting is always open?

- Journal if you have entered His door.

- What did you see and/or hear?

- Was it a risk for you to enter?

- Do you frequent meeting with Him?

- What does this verse mean to you?

"For a day in Your courts is better than a thousand outside. I would rather stand at the threshold of the house of my God than dwell in the tents of wickedness"
(Psalm 84:10 NASB).

Prayer

Lord God, allow me to walk in Your marvelous light. I want Your kingdom to shine through me for others to see.

ENCOUNTER

Avenger Angels

Often on a very busy morning, with various matters to take care of is when Papa God decides to bring an epiphany experience to us. On such a day, I head out my door, determined to make a quick stop at my bank, complete a single transaction inside, get back into my car and head straight to home. I don't have a lot of extra time to spare, so no additional stops will take place this trip.

Parking my car at the bank, I set my keys on the passenger seat and start to reach in the back for my paperwork. Suddenly without warning I hear the familiar sound of all four car doors locking. My first reaction is how did this happen? The keys are not touching anything. Only my keys are situated on the passenger seat. My hands aren't close to the lock buttons. This is absurd. I am puzzled and at a loss for an explanation.

Because I am curious, I hit the unlock button and try the driver's door. As soon as I attempt to open the door, the security alarm blares its distinctive clamoring noise. Now the keys are desperately needed. Feeling unnerved because of the noise, and knowing others might be checking my car, I grab my keys and mistakenly hit the "panic" button. Cessation of this offensively loud blast does not happen. With an all-or-nothing feeling I frantically spot the unlock button and click it. Silence. Ah, wonderful silence.

Relieved, I lean back in the driver's seat and try to relax. As soon as I get my composure I will head into the bank and take care of my transactions. But I think about the doors suddenly locking and deep within me the thought arises. Oh, oh. I have a feeling I'm going to need to remain in my car for some time.

Out of the corner of my eye I am aware of movement in the passenger seat. As I turn my head to look, I am conscious of a presence occupying the space. What is this? Even as I think that, I hear a voice saying "take a good look at what you are about to see." Past encounters with angels have taught me to realize one or more of them are constantly with me, even when I am not fully cognizant of them.

I look closely at the angelic presence in my car. He appears to be wearing an Avengers suit. Surprised and a bit taken aback, I giggle at the sight of an angel in a costume. Holy Spirit hears my giggle and the Avenger suit is suddenly gone. "You have seen correctly," Holy Spirit informs me. "This one is among the myriad of angels which have come to avenge the false teachings that the Bride of Christ has been convinced of."

I react instantly. "But Jesus' blood was given to avenge every wrong done to us." "Yes," Holy Spirit concurs, "but the Body of Christ has come into a stagnant place." That saddens me. I don't want to hear that the church is standing still. "She has believed that it is her responsibility to do something to inherit eternal life. Many in the Church believe it is up to man to prove him or herself to Father for acceptance. They don't understand His glorious unconditional love."

"Papa God," I call out, "You have an abundant life for each one of us. Help us recognize that our relationship with You and Your Son is what Jesus has already paid the ultimate price for on the cross. It is finished."

"Closely observe what I am about to show you," Holy Spirit continues. Immediately my eyes are open to see angels on rooftops, other angels standing guard at doorways, many angels perched on windowsills, and countless angels escorting people to their destinations. All of them have swords at their sides and helmets on their heads. They appear as I imagine a Roman Legionnaire looked in biblical times, on guard and patrolling his conquered territory. Holy Spirit's words are enlightening. "These are angels sent ahead of Father's beloved Bride of Christ, to guard each of you along the way and to bring you to the place Father has prepared."

I understand that the place He has prepared is not heaven in the future. Heaven is here on earth as we live and carry the Kingdom of God within us. Holy Spirit tells me, "This place Father has prepared is the place of rest, a place where striving, anxiety, and stress has been removed, a place of complete acceptance, assurance, comfort, and freedom. It is rest in the finished work of Jesus Christ on the cross. The avenger angels are sent by Father to minister to His beloved the freedom that has already been won." I let out a sigh. My body and spirit are both reacting to the relief Holy Spirit's words bring. "The angels are cutting away counterintuitive teachings and the chains of bondage these teachings bring. They are guarding minds and cutting off the spiritual blinders. The avenger angels are spearing condemning words before they are spoken, either verbally or thoughtfully."

I look again at the many angels I see in my range of sight. On each of their shields is a star illuminating brightly. "Jesus is the Bright Morning Star. He is the Light of the gospel." The words flow melodiously from Holy Spirit. As He declares this, large streaks of colors in the atmosphere begin appearing. The colors dance and twirl in response to His words. His statement of truth expresses His love for Jesus. Soon the sky is a mural of exquisite colors, blending together. All creation acknowledges Jesus.

"Now come with Me and I will show you more," Holy Spirit adds.

I am lifted high above the earth, gazing down at it. The formations of the continents are clear to me as the earth rotates and each land mass comes into view. What amazes me as I observe the earth is all the star-like intense bright lights that are shining from the lands. I am thinking He has taken me above the stars, and the lights I see are a portion of the celestial body below. But it is daylight. The stars are above me and not evident yet. "What you are seeing is the myriad of angels that have been assigned to bring full knowledge of the New Covenant relationship between Father and all of you that He so deeply desires." I remember the shield of each angel having a star on it. From high above the earth, I can see the illuminated energy generated by the angels as they go about working on their assignment.

"At various times and seasons people will come into the understanding of the truth which Father is communicating to the Bride of Christ," Holy Spirit declares. "It is happening now with many but will escalate as greater numbers begin to share from their hearts the reality of the revelation. Those who have not yet entered the Kingdom of God will understand fully without being encumbered by previous teachings the moment they walk through the open door into His Kingdom life."

Suddenly, as if being prompted by what Holy Spirit has just said, the stars on the shield of each angel on earth emit a brilliance that reaches into the heavenlies. "Why is the light from the shields so heightened?" I ask. "Each avenger angel in unison has lifted his shield. They are in complete agreement with the words I have spoken" Holy Spirit answers me.

Immediately the atmosphere becomes alive with the brilliance from their stars. I can hear a heavenly cadence bringing about rhythmic movement. I feel a shift and a change. I sense the spirit of God within many people is being awakened to the amazing truth that Jesus came to abolish and fulfill the law which none of us can do.

"I have one more thing to show you. Let's go back," he tells me. "But I love it here" I respond. "Can we stay? I want to weave through the brilliance of the angels' stars and hear the cadence as it intensifies. Can this place be harnessed and brought to earth for all to see and experience?"

"You will hear and see it." I feel us descend until I am once again sitting inside my car. "What are you noticing now?" He asks me. "I see some of the angels begin to accelerate their work. It looks as if others are still standing guard, waiting for their cue".

"As hearts are prepared, Father increases each angel's assignment" Holy Spirit continues. "The change is being expedited. Creation waits in eager expectation for the children of God to be revealed. Together, every one of you, Beloved bride of Christ, will dance with joy in one accord!"

I take one more look around to see a large number of avenger angels. I am in my car, needing to go into the bank. However, my spirit has been so energized by what I've been shown that I want to step out of my car and suddenly burst forth in a dance of eager expectation.

But I'll wait so I can dance in unison with the Body of Christ from that wondrous place of rest!

As I walk into the bank, my angel is with me.

"For if there had been nothing wrong with that first covenant, no place would have been sought for another. But God found fault with the people and said: "The days are coming, declares the Lord, when I will make a new covenant with the people of Israel and with the people of Judah. For I will forgive their wickedness and will remember their sins no more." By calling this covenant 'new,' He has made the first one obsolete; and what is obsolete and outdated will soon disappear" (Hebrews 8:7-8; 12-13 NIV).

"I, Jesus, have sent My angel to testify to you these things for the churches. I am the root and the descendant of David, the bright morning star"
(Revelation 22:16 NIV).

Points to Ponder

- Do you think of angels as being avenger angels?
- If so, what battles do you feel they are or have been involved in?
- Do you feel you have to prove yourself to God for Him to accept you?
- Have you witnessed the victories/the freedom?

Prayer

Papa God, prepare my heart so that I can participate in the angels' assignments. I want to be a part of the expedited change here on earth and in the Heavenly realm. Show me what I must do as Your child so that I too can be included as part of Your Beloved Bride and dance with joy united with the Body of Christ.

ENCOUNTER

Volunteer Nurse

A commentator on the news said the governor of Florida is calling for 1000 volunteer nurses. He is speaking to the predicted devastation of another new hurricane to make landfall.

"I wish I was a nurse" I told my husband after hearing the governor's plea. "I would be there in a heartbeat to help."

Apparently, Papa God had been listening and sent an angel to me. I felt her firmly tug at the back of my jeans which compelled me to turn and see she was moving out to the street in front of my house. My legs burst into a run behind her as she swiftly moved. It felt as if we were on a runway gathering speed before takeoff. She extended her right hand out behind her. I grabbed it as we began to pass over my city.

We rapidly crossed over water. Countless angels covered in gold were raising their swords above us as we passed through. The gate guarded by the angels into the protected access point of the heavenly atmosphere had been opened for us. My angel firmly took hold of my hand, and we made our way onto a heap of rubble in what looked like a war zone. "Where are we?" I inquired. I heard nothing from her.

Collapsed buildings, concrete pieces everywhere, glass, debris, power-lines, and a few exacerbated people wandering around in a daze was the scene before my eyes. A portion of a crumbled sign which read "Revolution" was sticking out from the piles of debris. I assumed I was in Cuba which had just been hit by the fierce hurricane.

The sound of groaning and crying increased and became almost more than I could bear. "Please tell me what to do!" I called out in desperation to Papa God.

"Ayuda! Ayuda! Ayuda!" I know very little of the Spanish language, but I did comprehend the despair in the voice I heard.

The angel led me to a man lying in the street, covered in dust and bleeding profusely. He looked me in the eye and my spirit screamed out "I don't know what I am doing!" But the angel brought me a huge bag which she opened to show an enormous supply of tourniquets, IV lines, and packets of blood.

Emergency teams were desperately working to save lives. One man with a medical cross on his shirt spoke to me in English. "Quick! This man needs a transfusion. Use type O." I needed to be confident in what I was to do and felt a slight panic as I proceeded to find a blood vessel and insert the intravenous line. Thankfully using my English words and sharing with this wounded man how much Jesus loves him, did not seem to be a barrier. His eyes told me that he heard my words in his language. I placed the blood supply bag on a pile of concrete and ran to the next person covered in blood. Daylight quickly became dusk and then darkness repeated itself as I persevered daily, continuing to administer help to so many wounded and scared persons. Each person I approached had an aura of light shining on them. I understood the light was an awesome sign of Papa God dispelling the dark cloud of sorrow and giving me His strength. Miracles were happening before my eyes. The supply of blood and the IV lines never diminished in number. There was always more than enough.

I have never given anyone a blood transfusion. Surprisingly I was not tired, but was shocked to realize I had helped while not having any expertise or skill in what I was doing. A clear audible voice spoke through the hushed air. "You can do all things through Christ which strengthens you." It was the angel who had not spoken to me until now. "Yes, I have my Papa God who equips me and allows me to be used by Him."

I asked her what her name was. "Rakak" she told me with a slight smile. "Why am I here?" Rakak readily replies "*I AM* heard you speak your desire to support and assist. Help was needed here at the moment you spoke your desire. You were willing and He sent me to travel with you. *I AM* is always able to give you all that you need."

I knew I hadn't done enough. Having seen the devastation in my own state from a destructive hurricane, I wanted to do more! I needed to do more! But Papa God quieted my spirit. He had once again shown me His love, His provision, His compassion and how we are naturally supernatural because of Jesus Christ.

Rakak lovingly transported me back to my home, over the water and through the lifted gates that the angels in gold permanently surround and guard. I looked at the clock. It had been only ten minutes since I spoke the words to my husband. And yet I was there in the spirit administering help for many days

.

"But my God shall supply all your need according to His riches in glory by Christ Jesus"
(Philippians 4:19 KJV).

"For with God nothing shall be impossible"
(Luke 1:37 KJV).

Points to Ponder

- Do you feel God knows when your heart desires to be helpful in a situation?
- How do you think you would react if an angel took you to a location where help was needed, leading you to help with something unfamiliar, and supplied you with everything you required?

Prayer

Father God, thank You that You give me, Your trustworthy one the strength to serve You. Cause others to see You through my response of love.

Help With Prayer

Angels help with healing. They can physically show in detail how Holy Spirit is directing us to pray and declare. It seems a bit strange, but a friend called asking for prayer that her mother's elimination system would start working. She had been in the hospital for some time and was not able to be released to go home unless her bowels were functioning properly. I saw in a vision an angel massaging her kidneys. Explaining to my friend what I saw, she exclaimed that she didn't know angels could touch organs inside a body!

We prayed the vision the Lord had shown, and her mother was released the next day!

Angels can accomplish any task God calls them to do. Sometimes God's angels are visually showing what needs to be declared for His healing to manifest.

"For I will restore health unto thee, and I will heal thee of thy wounds, saith the Lord"
(Jeremiah 30:17 KJV).

"Look at the birds of the air; they do not sow or reap or store away in barns, and yet your heavenly Father feeds them. Are you not much more valuable than they?"
(Matthew 6:26 NIV).

Points to Ponder

- Do you believe Papa God can show you specifically what needs to be healed in a person?
- Have you had this experience to pray what you see?
- What are the results?

Prayer

Papa God, I want to serve and be of assistance to You and those in need of healing. Will You reveal and show me specifically how to partner with You and the angels to minister to those clearly in need?

Golden Passage

"Look at those stately, distinctive green trees lining either side of the path I am on," I say to myself. Each branch is full of blossoms emitting a sweet fragrance suggesting what the aroma of heaven might be.

Ahead of me is a fountain of crystalline, sparkling water. When I study the sight, it appears the water dances in the fountain. I remember my childhood and the joy of being in a water fountain splashing, laughing, and having the cool water tickling my feet. Where am I? I try to grasp all that I am viewing, but I know I need to move on and discover what is ahead.

The path is red cobblestone. A thick rim of gold outlines each stone. Rings of gold form a ripple pattern, pushing gold out onto the path as I take steps forward. I'm on a golden passage to somewhere unknown.

The path turns and I see an angel sitting on a bench of gold. Gold is everywhere! I've seen this angel before. She is wearing an exquisite dress. The jewels, fabric, and style must be luxuriously designed specifically for her. She rises. Her white dress brings thoughts of a Viennese waltz. Every movement causes the dress to flow in splendor. She approaches me, smiling a familiar smile. It feels good to be close to her again. She brushes the train of her dress across me, and I am enveloped in a glorious, swirling array of fluorescent colors. The angel is beside me. Has there been a sharp change in elevation? My legs become wobbly and weak. I'm wondering if I will stumble and fall. She reaches out to steady me.

The sheets of colors continue to whirl above and around me until they become mixed together as one lustrous color. I've read there are over 5000 colors we see, but this is something new. The color is swirling closer, drawing me into this vibrant coloration. With shortened breath, I ask her "What color is this?"

Truth tenderly flows from her lips "This is the true color of *I AM*. You are experiencing how the visible and invisible colors, hues, color values, are perfectly completed together as one in His Glory."

Curiously I reach to touch the color of *I AM* surrounding me. A soothing feeling of trust fills me as I observe myself becoming entirely transformed into this undefinable color. Asking the angel beside me what has happened to me she replies "This is who you are. This color is called The Bride of Christ."

I think how difficult it often is for the majority of His sons and daughters to see ourselves as Papa God sees us.

"Watch what happens," she tells me.

With the train of her dress in hand, she pirouettes as a ballet dancer, creating what looks like a hole or gate in the atmosphere for men, women, and children to enter into the perfect color of the Bride of Christ. Coming through this entrance are thousands upon thousands of persons colored in blue, followed by multitudes in yellow, countless numbers in green. Masses of people in orange and red are entering. Huge numbers in purple, gold, silver, and a variety of colors move in through the opening.

"These are those that see themselves with one or more characteristics of *I AM*. They are content to be operating and sharing in the characteristics of God they recognize. Jesus desires to draw all even deeper into the knowledge of Him and their true identity in Him."

"Will we ever realize we are capable of being the color of the completed Bride of Christ?"

"Watch again." She moves the people together. Their colors begin to swirl and blend. It is the plan of *I AM* for you to need each other. As you come together, receiving insight and understanding from each other, you link up and unify, becoming the color of Jesus Himself. The Bride of Christ is your color."

Each person looks at themselves, discovering they are the new color of the strikingly beautiful Bride. I deeply take in the loveliness of the sight of the completed Bride of Christ. What a glorious display of the heart of Papa God. As one voice, we break out in praise and thanksgiving to Him who was, who is, and who is to come! We are divinely connected. We are so diverse, yet so one united in Him.

We're listening intently as the angel declares "This is how Jesus sees

His Bride. Not fragmented, but wholly, securely interlinked, and interlocked. Now come with me to the fountain" she says, leading us all on the path back to the dancing waters.

"Jump in."

We hesitate. "Don't be afraid. Your identity in Him does not change nor wash away. The water is sweetest in the fountain. The abundant love of *I AM* is everlasting. Immerse yourselves in relationship with Jesus."

We splash in the fountain. Laughter fills the air. We embrace each other. Love binds us together. Sitting in the pool of water, we begin sharing our experiences of knowing Jesus. Eyes are opened, revelation is flowing. Eagerness to know, understand, and experience more is increasing. The color of the Bride of Christ is dazzling in the Fountain of Life!

The angel has been observing us as we draw closer to Jesus and to each other. She nods as if hearing a command. Holding the train of her dress once again, she pirouettes over us with a soft breeze. We find ourselves standing together on the cobblestone path. As we move, liquid gold flows out onto the path. I just must exclaim excitedly "We are on the golden passage!"

She waves a banner over us. It reads:

"I will give you every place where you set your foot, as I promised Moses" (Joshua 1:3 NIV).

Together we raise our hands high in excitement as the banner confirms our heart's cry for Holy Spirit to move through us, calling the earth into true relationship with Jesus. Does the angel see our reaction to the banner? We all look for her as the banner hovers over us, but she is gone.

Deeper Revelation

Being with the Body of Christ is blissful. There is coming a day when the Bride of Christ's color will permeate the earth. Our senses are becoming aware of this extraordinary, magnificent color beginning to settle on us, transforming Papa God's people into unity with Him and one another.

I saw a television commercial promoting a car manufacturer. "Together we are better than we are alone." I wonder if the company realizes they are professing Papa God's heart?

"To know You is to experience a flowing fountain, drinking in Your life, springing up to satisfy. In the light of Your holiness, we receive the light of revelation" (Psalm 36:9 TPT).

Points to Ponder

- What feelings or thoughts come to your mind when your eyes capture intense, vibrant colors?
- Highlight a personal experience and your reaction when this has happened to you.
- List some definitive words when you see or imagine a sparkling, dancing body of water.

Prayer

Father God, take me deep into Your refreshing, effervescent, colorful river of life and goodness.

ENCOUNTER

Morning Sky

The morning sky is clear and sparkling like an unending angelic blue crystal. It's calming for me to keep gazing upward, and delightful to hear the undisturbed sound of chirping birds.

Many friends have said the current chaotic unrest in our society is intense and has taken away their joy. Hearing this saddens me greatly.

Taking a deep breath of outside air to refresh me, I spot movement to my right. Figures in glowing pink color are approaching me. As they come closer, I recognize two of the beings as the same angels I have encountered previously. The exquisite beauty and heavenly pink light being emitted from each of the many angels is captivating. Gracefully moving, they become a company of angels encompassing me in the brilliance of the light they carry. Radiant pink light penetrates deep into the pores of my skin in their presence.

Experiencing this awesome, unexpected heavenly appointment, I watch as the company of angels begin dancing and praising around me. The supernatural sound of a finely tuned symphony orchestra fills the atmosphere with a resounding celebration. Pure colors in various hues flash around me as far as my eyes can see. The fusion of sweet-sounding musical instruments ebbs and flows. I'm observing the angels' profound relationship with this heavenly music as they twirl, leap, bow, ascend, and descend in glorious synchronization with the music and each other. Before me is an eloquently designed ballet of splendor.

I wonder if I am allowed to ask a question while the angels are expressing such supreme joy in their ballet. I am quiet, but they smile and nod. Holy Spirit must have relayed my thoughts.

"Why are you dancing before me?"

One of the two I recognize answers me. "We are expressing the Order of Heaven. *I AM* is Sovereign. The host of heaven surrounds the sovereignty of *I AM*. This is His story, His melody, His dance."

The elegant ballet continues. May it never end in my sight.

Deeper Revelation

I am immersed completely in this encounter. My emotions and senses respond. My heart cries out for all of humanity to be drawn into the theater of heaven, encountering our majestic Triune God. May all people experience and savor the magnificence of His story through His ballet of love, peace and tranquility.

"When anxiety was great within me, Your consolation brought me joy"
(Psalm 94:19 NIV).

"Let them praise his name with dancing, making melody to him with tambourine and lyre"
(Psalm 149:3 ESV).

"And David danced before the Lord with all his might…"
(2 Samuel 6:14 ESV).

"Then shall the young women rejoice in the dance, and the young men and the old shall be merry. I will turn their mourning into joy; I will comfort them, and give them gladness for sorrow"
(Jeremiah 31:13-14 ESV).

Points to Ponder

- Have you experienced the magnificence of His story?
- Do you know that you are in His story?

Prayer

Father God, my heart cries out for You. Draw me into the theater of heaven and allow me to experience the magnificence of Your story.

SMALL SIGHTINGS

Great Is The Lord

Upstairs in a meeting room of a church, I am to speak at, I am praying for an upcoming meeting. "How Great is Our God" is being played and sung downstairs by the song leaders of the event.

I quietly join in worship, but as I do, I notice the meeting room door opens and an entire contingency of huge angels comes marching shoulder to shoulder into the room with a cadence of perfect unison to the beat of the song. The angels march towards me, circle me, and continue on, marching back out the same door as the worship downstairs lingers.

The angels are drawn to the place where How Great is Our God is being professed through song in worshiping hearts! Times in worship will cause Holy Spirit to take us from one spiritual level to another.

"Draw near to God and He will draw near to you…"
(James 4:8 ESV).

"But may all who seek you rejoice and be glad in you; may those who love your salvation say continually, Great is the Lord!"
(Psalm 40:16 ESV).

"Exalt the Lord our God! Bow low before His feet, for He is holy!"
(Psalm 99:5 NLT).

"He is your praise, He is your God, who has done for you these great and awesome things which your eyes have seen"
(Deuteronomy 10:21 NKJV).

Points to Ponder

- Have you had an experience of hearing a heavenly choir worshiping God and been drawn to worship with them?

- Why do you think our worship draws the angels?

Prayer

Father God, may my worship of You also draw the angels to join me in song. Allow me to hear the heavenly choir worshiping You.

ENCOUNTER

Twirling

When Holy Spirit talks to two friends in different states on the same day about getting together, it needs to happen! Airline fares and availability were, of course, ready for my friend to capture. She came shortly after Holy Spirit's direction to stay a few days with me and reminisce of previous times together and enjoy the presence of the Lord as we have done during so many occasions before.

After picking her up at the airport we had a fun adventure finding a place for lunch. The menu cover showed what appeared to be wings and the number five was mentioned several times by the restaurant chef. Discussing the possible symbolic meaning of the number five and the wings on our drive to my house, we concluded we had no direct answer. That evening she and I were eager to share our love for Jesus and the exciting life we are living with Him. Settling in, grateful for our special gift of God's anointed time, we both simultaneously sensed a large angel was with us. My friend saw him holding a cruet of oil or water, walking towards us. She presumed he was approaching us to splash the oil or water on me. However, he didn't move further, but appearing to have received a precise command, stood very still. At the time she was sharing I saw another angel in a corner of the room. This angel was twirling what appeared to be a female angel. His right arm was high, carefully holding her extended left arm and hand. He twirled her gently, tenderly, around and around. They were not dancing, instead it seemed to be just the symbolic expression of Papa God's love. My friend and I both were questioning what we were witnessing. We were thankful but not understanding the significance of this encounter. As we soaked in His presence, we asked Holy Spirit to clarify what we saw and why we experienced it.

Taking a freshly brewed cup of coffee in our hands the following morning, we began sharing how inquisitive we both were about the angels God had sent. Thanking God for the morning dew sparkling on the grass outside, the birds singing their songs of praise, and the heat of the sun warming the day we pressed on to inquire of the Lord. Noticing movement, we observed the same large angel standing on the outside of a clear glass door where we were seated inside on either side of a table. "Should I open the door and let him in," I asked my friend. It seemed to be a silly question since we both knew he could instantly be inside without the door being accessed. But there was also a bit of abnormal hesitancy with my question. He stood there patiently. Standing up, taking a step toward the door, I reached for the handle and opened the door for our awaiting angel. We didn't see him enter or move closer to us. Immediately he was standing in front of my friend holding the cruet of oil in his hand. Tipping the cruet, he began pouring the oil on her head, allowing it to run down her body, covering her in the holy oil, just as it was on Aaron's head, beard, and robe. (Psalm 133). What a glorious sight to be able to share with her. "I feel it! I feel the oil on me! I felt it before you said anything," she exclaimed.

I opened my mouth to confirm again what we both were seeing, but Papa God had a specific love message for her. His words prophetically began to flow out of me to her. I'm not including the personal word God gave her, but she stated over and over that it was life-changing. We were in awe how God presented us with the angel the night before and how the angel waited for God's perfect timing the next morning when he manifested his assignment given from God's heart.

We had some fun activities to be involved in during the day, and talked about desiring three of our close friends to be included on a video call in the evening. We are a group of five, brought together by the sovereignty of God and sealed by the blood of Jesus. We've experienced much with God, Jesus, Holy Spirit and angels through the years. Our small tight-knit group longed once again to be united. Plans worked out just as we had prayed they would. All five of us were available for the call that evening.

Mealtime of garden veggies and a tasty chicken dish was over. Time to clean up dishes and head outside to arrange chairs and camera for our video meet-up. My friend and I were set. As we prayed for Holy Spirit's anointing on our time, we were aware that the angel had been waiting outside at the bottom of the deck's steps. What is your name, we questioned him. His strong declaration "Deliverer" answered us. But Jesus is our deliverer. Did we mishear his answer? With clarity and assurance from Holy Spirit, we were graciously reminded a deliverer is one who delivers, and that's exactly what the angel named Deliverer had done earlier.

We excitedly greeted everyone on our call. It was exceptional to be back with each other. The conversation started by describing our unique lunchtime, the wings on the menu, and the number five. We shared of the angel's appearance the previous night, and how Deliverer waited overnight to pour the oil over my friend. She shared the impactful word she received. I spoke about the angel twirling a female angel in the corner of the room. Papa God revealed the female angel represented each of us individually. As I was sharing, one specific angel for each of us was taking both of our hands, turning us to face him, and smiling sweetly with the love of Jesus radiating from his eyes into ours. Each angel then mouthed the words "Jesus loves you" to the one he was holding. No spoken words were heard. We felt the touch of Jesus' perfect love being given to us.

Our assigned angel took our right hand with his right hand, lifted our arms and began to lightly, gently twirl us. As we continued to softly twirl, as if ballerinas turning pirouette style, Holy Spirit revealed we are not encumbered. We are feather-like, light, without the burdens of the world on or in us. Everything that had entangled us had been released in the twirling. "You are free" were the words of God. "Freedom! Freedom! Freedom!" the five angels called out.

What an amazing, majestic God of love embraces us! We thanked Him for using His angels to bring His messages, for Him orchestrating His perfect time for us to be gathered in one accord, for speaking in numerous ways and not being silent, and for how relentless His love is for us. Gratitude and overwhelming worship filled our hearts.

One of the friends looked up the word twirl. To our joy and confirmation, she read "twirl: to spin lightly and quickly around, especially repeatedly."

"We are feather-like without entanglement, free to spread our spiritual wings and soar with wings as eagles"
(Isaiah 40:31, NLT).

"Now the Lord is the Spirit, and where the Spirit of the Lord is, there is freedom"
(2 Corinthians 3:17 NIV).

"But they that wait upon the Lord shall renew their strength. They shall mount up with wings like eagles; they shall run and not be weary; they shall walk and not faint"
(Isaiah 40:31 TLB).

Points to Ponder

- Have there been coincidences that amaze you about the perfect timing of God playing out?

- What do the scriptural words "free to spread our spiritual wings and sour as eagles" mean to you?

- Reflect and meditate on the value of the moments you realize God's faithfulness is working on your behalf.

Prayer

Holy Spirit reveal to me the areas of my life where I am entangled. I want to dance unencumbered with You in total freedom. I want to experience being feather-like, light, and without the burdens of the world on me. Because of who You are, Jesus, help me to release what needs to be released so I can hear You say, "You are free!"

ENCOUNTER

Ballet Of Love

She is outside my window. I see her twirling on her toes, just as a graceful ballerina does. She dances effortlessly, as if being one with a poem of love.

It is an odd sight. I watch with curiosity as one ballerina becomes two. Their exquisite, flowing pink dresses sparkle in the sunlight. I become acutely aware that they have been sent by my Papa God.

"What are they dancing for?" I ask Papa God.

"I am playing the music of your heart for the angels. They hear the love and worship coming from deep within you and they respond to the rhythm your perpetual worship produces."

"Is my heart continuously singing to Jesus even when I am not aware of it?" As I watch the two angels pirouette together, my voice joins my heart song. Praising and extolling the Triune God is powerful.

The angels bow and leap for joy in their dance as my heart expresses gratitude to Jesus. Watching them reminds me of reading about new wireless technology that can detect peoples' emotions by their breathing and heart rate. This is just science catching up to Papa God. He knows us and hears the song of our heart without us saying a word.

"Can I join the angels, or am I to watch?"

Graciously Papa God answers me. "Your heart is their source of music. Go out and dance with them."

I am hesitant to go outside and start dancing. I open the door a little, then swing the door wide open, being drawn to the glorious sound of celestial singing.

The angels are waiting for me. A feeling of tenderness and devotion envelopes me as they take my hands. Together we dance before the Throne of Grace. They encourage me to twirl. Jubilation fills my spirit and soul. I know I am dancing my poem of love to Jesus!

"Praise the Lord! Praise God in His sanctuary; praise Him in His mighty heavens! Praise Him for His mighty deeds; praise Him according to His excellent greatness! Praise Him with trumpet sound; praise Him with lute and harp! Praise Him with tambourine and dance; praise Him with strings and pipe! Praise Him with sounding cymbals; praise Him with loud clashing cymbals! Let everything that has breath praise the Lord!"
(Psalm 150:1-6 ESV).

"Sing to Him, sing praises to Him, tell of all His wonderful works"
(Psalm 105:2 ESV).

Points to Ponder

- What is the music of your heart?
- Explain what that means to you.
- When Jesus feels the music of your heart what emotions do you think He feels?

Prayer

Jesus, I am filled with songs of Your love, joy, and freedom. I long to dance with the angels before You, praising You with my poem of love for You. May my dance and my heart's song be pleasing to You.

SMALL SIGHTINGS

Pink Ballet Pointe Shoes

A few of us are at a Christian retreat together, engaged in worshiping Jesus, hearing Him speak, and receiving His love. As some are lying or sitting on the floor, an angel appears and encircles each one of us, one at a time. He is in pink ballet pointe shoes. The pink shoes tend to reflect much of the light around him. He is very graceful and purposeful. He makes a full circle around each of us with smooth ballet movements. He is expressing God's language without words as he turns, rises up, and jumps among us. This angel appears to feel the energy and the emotion of his dance. We understand a ballet will convey an atmosphere, a theme, a story. He is conveying a change in the atmosphere we live in. As we ponder the sight of a ballerina angel in pink ballet pointe shoes, the atmosphere outside becomes electrically charged with sudden, physical crackling bolts of lightning, explosive thunder, and whipping wind which seems to cause the room to vibrate. Awe struck and speechless we are aware that our holy God is speaking through the natural elements of this storm. We feel empowered and enclosed by His Presence. Thanking Him for sending His angel and for the natural storm confirming what He is deliberately doing in the spirit realm, we respond in praise for the change He is bringing.

"The voice of the Lord is over the waters; the God of glory thunders; the Lord is over many waters. The voice of the Lord is powerful; the voice of the Lord is full of majesty."
(Psalm 29:3-4 NKJV).

Points to Ponder

- Thunder and lightning at Mt. Sinai were prominent as God descended to speak to Moses. (see Exodus 10-20 NIV). Find other scriptural passages of thunder and lightning.

- Do we in this day consider God's voice roaring through thunder?

Prayer

Father God, teach me to be sensitive to the changes in the natural atmosphere so I can be more aware of what You are doing and what is happening in the spiritual realm.

ENCOUNTER

Floor Encounter

I've laid on the floor many times, for many reasons during my early years of talking to God and growing spiritually. Back then, playing the cassette tapes with plenty of volume caused my spirit to sing, and filled the room with Christian music. I'd bow down in reverence as I sang the words to the song "I love You Lord, and I lift my voice, to worship You, oh my soul rejoice." I'd feel the breath of angels joining me, adding their worship to mine. I didn't know angels could be so close, but the feeling was real and tangible.

Lying prostrate with my face down, not caring if I was able to breathe or not, my spirit longed to reverently worship Jesus. I was reaching out to Him, not asking for answers, only desperately yearning for the One my heart desired. An overpowering awareness of the absolute holiness and majesty of Jesus gained control of my thoughts and I told myself I am undeserving of being in His presence. The floor seemed too elevated for me to come before Him. I felt I must be spiritually low, far beneath the carpeted surface to be in the company of the King of Kings, Son of God, Holy and Righteous One, Savior of the World, Messiah!

I wrestled with the floor, struggling to spiritually lower myself until finally feeling it was okay with my spirit. Being as low as I could possibly be enabled my tears to flow freely. My heart held on to the hope that Jesus would receive my overwhelming gratitude and would accept and meet me.

Angels appeared and gently held my hands, wanting to assure me. But being low under the floor surface satisfied my (false) perception of being unworthy to receive all the love God says He continuously lavishes on me. I needed Jesus, to personally speak to me, saying I am justified in God's sight to approach the holy Throne of Grace.

An intense effort to breathe came over me. Was I fearful? Was this apprehension? Time seemed to be standing still. This was so strange. I was not able to identify what was happening.

Without delay a peaceful calm invaded my emotions. Deep within me I sensed a flame was ignited in my spirit, reaching upwards, touching Jesus. The unmistakable voice of Jesus tenderly spoke to me. "Rise up! Come here My beloved! You are forever the cherished treasure of My heart."

Rising in response to Jesus, I was completely wrapped in the loving embrace of His arms. He canceled my uncertainty. He called me honored, valuable, and worthy! Heaven's angels encircled me, filling the room's atmosphere with their presence and their voices lifted in worship. I felt one of the angels place a soft, warm covering over me. I wanted to wrap it around myself and snuggle in the confidence and security it brought me. An awesome peace consumed any doubts I previously had.

Knowing, believing, and walking in His truth that I am His still fills me with indescribable true joy. I just can't stop saying the name of Jesus and continuously giving my holy, magnificent God the glory due His name!

He loves us unconditionally. Old, false beliefs are replaced with the knowledge we are made in God's image and our identity is in Him. Sometimes you just need a floor encounter with God and His angels to understand the truth of who and whose you are!

"For by grace you have been saved through faith. And this is not your own doing; it is the gift of God"
(Ephesians 2:8 ESV).

"So then, the law was our guardian until Christ came, in order that we might be justified by faith"
(Galatians 3:24 ESV).

Points to Ponder

- What does 'justified because of Jesus' mean to you?
- Have you experienced floor encounters with God and/or His angels?

Prayer

Papa God, remind me that I am Your beloved one. Show me how favored and blessed with Your grace and spiritual blessings I am because I am in Christ.

ENCOUNTER

Approaching Carriage

"Papa God, will You cultivate my heart so that I can bear Your Presence even more" is my sincere prayer today. Those dust balls on the floors can be mopped away later. I just want to be silent, listening for Papa God to speak to me. I sense many angels are surrounding me, putting a sheer translucent cloth over me, and separating me from the distracting things in the natural. They are ministering to me because God heard my cry to experience Him once again in an overwhelming way.

I am suddenly placed in the midst of a crowd of people spanning many city blocks. I'm unable to see anything other than the backsides of people clamoring to obtain a perfect vantage point to see what the commotion is about. The tremendous amount of anticipation in the atmosphere is tangibly felt. Why all this excitement?

Clip clop, clip clop, the rhythmic sound of hoof beats, of approaching horses is intense. I stand on my tip toes to see sixteen powerful, strong, majestic creatures. They have big chests and are extremely muscular. High, white plums adorn their head stalls, white blankets are over their backs. Each horse has a gold and silver breast collar. I'm stunned by the resplendence of these horses. The workmanship of what they are wearing looks like nothing I have ever seen before. These horses are breathtakingly distinctive in their magnificence, much more than any show horse ever could be!

Behind the horses is a spectacular carriage, elaborately decorated, gilded, and fit for a reigning monarch. Who is in the carriage? With precision the horses come to a stop. I am close enough that I see a heralder holding a brass coronation style trumpet. The angels tell me the trumpet has been hand crafted for this particular heralder.

Now standing on something high, the heralder takes his trumpet, puts it to his lips and blows a clarion call that all can hear. In a loud voice he announces "Hear ye, hear ye. The king has been summoned by the cry of his people's hearts and is responding to the call. Your Majesty, Your Honorable King has arrived!"

My heart throbs. I'm feeling the surroundings spinning and I'm losing my balance. Grabbing hold of the unsuspecting one next to me before I fall helps me from fainting. I'm sorry I tell her. I'll be okay. Who is this king? I have never been in the presence of a royal king before. My feet are frozen to the ground. The intensity of the moment has me locked in place.

The doorman who has been guarding the entrance of the carriage steps forward and opens the carriage door. A blazing illumination encompasses the interior of the carriage. Darkness cannot exist there. The doorman kindly, carefully extends his hand, assisting the awaited king out the door and down the step. Breathing escapes me. The king stands before the crowd of people. His long white train flowing from his robe appears to be never-ending. Breathing ten times faster than I normally breathe, my chest crushing me, I focus on this royal magnificence and exquisite beauty one more time. The angels are surrounding me, watching my reaction. It's almost as if they know what will happen next.

The king turns and begins to walk in my direction. Occasionally I can get a good look at him. He passes through the crowd as they part, and toss rose petals before him. My heart cries longingly "if only I could see him better!'

A brilliant light radiating from him is coming closer as He slowly moves through the crowds, approaching me. Through the radiance of the light, I catch a glimpse of the grandeur of his royal robe. I hear the angels whisper the robe is a symbol of his truth to his people. Squinting my eyes to focus more clearly, I notice what looks like writing on his robe. Is that a mistake? I'm still too far away and unable to read it. Sparkling gemstones of unrivaled brilliance grace his crown in colors reflecting the light within them. The crown looks heavy but he carries it upon his head with such ease.

In his right hand the king is holding a very large, ornamented scepter. I'm telling myself that he must be a sovereign king who rules with power and authority.

I want to get closer, but I am afraid. I am not dressed appropriately. My hair is a mess. I have no makeup on. I'm only here to see why this awesome, royal person stopped and got out of his royal carriage among the crowded gathering.

As I contemplate this, I am aware that he is continuing to walk towards me. The closer he gets, the more brilliant the light emanating from him becomes. He is the only King of Light! I am not seeing the people around me anymore. Is the world slowing down? Are the people in slow motion? All I can see is HIM! My heart is beating so hard. Oh, but he won't be aware of me in this crowd I tell myself. Soon he'll pass me by and then I'll see the fullness of the train of his robe. I briefly catch sight of it. It is extremely lengthy, six servants of a sort are supporting the weight of the train. It extends considerably through the crowd. I'm unable to see its end.

My legs become weak. I am unable to stand. I collapse to the ground. The King of Light walks straight towards me. There's a quiet hush filling the air. What is happening? Oh my, what is happening? He is stopping right in front of me! He is turning. He is looking at me! Those eyes! That love! His love in His eyes is overwhelming me!

He knows me! He holds out His hand. He calls me by name! He says to me "Come away with Me, my beloved." I hesitate. Emphatically I tell him. "I can't go with you. I am not clean. I am not prepared." He holds out His hand. Passion is racing out of me to Him. I put my hand out and touch His. Instantly I am transformed!

I no longer have my old clothes on. I am beautiful. "You are altogether lovely" are His words to me. The dress I have on now is the most beautiful, stunning, glorious dress I have ever seen. It is white and it sparkles. I believe His words. I am altogether lovely.

He draws me out of the crowd and puts my arm through His. This is my Jesus! My Jesus! We begin walking towards the carriage. The angels are ahead of us, an angelic bodyguard team. Why are we doing this? We are leaving the people who came to see this king. Why?

We arrive at the carriage and are escorted into it. I sit with Him and He tenderly says "I have known you since before you were born." Suddenly my heart is completely captured, consumed, and enthralled with the King. He and I are sitting together sharing a great, divine exchange of soul-ravishing love!

I recognize how He has been dedicated to me since the day I was born. I can't seem to sit close enough to Him. I lean into Him as the carriage begins to move. I wonder, where are we going?

We travel a little, or maybe a lot. I don't know how far. I am just so taken by His deep, genuine love for me.

The carriage stops. The door is opened for us. We leave the carriage and walk up the steps into a magnificent palace. Jesus explains that this is my habitation of life with Him! Only He isn't saying it, He is singing it! He rejoices over me with singing!

The doors are opened, and I am looking into the palace. I am by myself now, but I know it is because He wants me to see something special. He has escorted me, but now He takes His rightful place.

Oh! A throne with a rainbow all around it. What beautiful colors. The Throne is immersed in flames. Fire, fire, fire. It's one continuous fire!

And seated at the throne is a person, glorious beyond words that I can describe. A sound like thunder is coming from this throne. The angels that were with me are now circled around the throne. I hear "Holy, Holy, Holy" continuously being exclaimed through song, reverberating in the atmosphere.

And there is my King! There is the love of my life. He is sitting at the right hand of His Father. He is bidding me to come to Him!

This is not forbidden ground. I have been invited. Jesus tells me that I may draw near to the throne. He says to me "Come confidently, fearlessly, and boldly. This is for you to share with me. Come!" I believe Him. I come to the Throne.

And to think that I may not have come on my own. I may have just looked at myself and not seen me the way my Jesus sees me. But when He held out his hand and touched me, I was changed.

Beloved Jesus, I desire to bring others here to gaze into Your loving eyes and to see Your holy Throne of beauty and grace!

Thank You for finding me in the crowd and calling me Your beloved. I sense the angels are celebrating the revelation I received.

Thank You, Papa God, for sending Your ministering angels to guide me into an understanding of how You pursue all of your family. Thank You that You are calling each of us to be a witness to those not yet believing in Your Son. May we step into our place in Your book. May Your Kingdom come, and Your will be done on earth as it is in heaven!

"As the Father has loved me, so have I loved you. Abide in my love"
(John 15:9 ESV).

"Because you are precious in My sight, you are honored and I love you"
(Isaiah 43:4 AMP).

"For you bless the righteous, O Lord; you cover them with a favor as with a shield"
(Psalm 5:12 ESV).

"But you, O Lord, are a shield about me, my glory, and the lifter of my head"
(Psalm 3:3 ESV).

Points to Ponder

- Do you feel deeply loved by Jesus? Or are you struggling to feel worthy to be loved by Him?
- Explain, using this symbolic encounter of the King and His carriage as an example.
- What does it mean for you to step into your place in God's book?

Prayer

Thank you Papa God that you call me precious and honored in your sight. King Jesus I desire to be with you even more every day.

ENCOUNTER

Car Transporter

"Slow down just a bit. I need to take a picture of this car transport trailer."

"What?" my husband reacts with curiosity. "We see so many of these on the highway. What's unique about this one?"

"I'm not sure yet."

Ah good. Got the picture. As we begin to pass the trailer I glance up at the white car in the front on the top row. Sitting in the driver's seat and turning to see me in my inquisitive state, is what appears to be a seemingly attentive, splendid looking angelic form. He acknowledges me.

"What are you doing riding in that car?" I ask him out loud. My husband turns his head, puzzled at me talking to the truck. Knowing it's unlawful for an individual to be riding in a vehicle loaded on one of these ramps, I'm very curious what I am witnessing.

As my curiosity peaks a translucent, mighty angel appears sitting in our back seat, leaning forward between my husband and me.

"I AM" he begins, "has summoned me to travel in a transporter trailer with a visual message in plain sight for all who will inquire. Many will pass and look up at the cars on board, but only a few will discern my presence as you have."

Looking directly at me he asks, "Will you share this message *I AM* is having me deliver?"

"Of course, I will." Papa God's goodness is always apparent as He sends His angels to bring words from His heavenly throne.

"The presence of *I AM* directs and counsels you through His wisdom. He leads you and provides Himself as your guide on your journeys."

Agreeing emphatically, I say "I believe and understand that. Being guided by Papa God comes about through relationship with Him. He is always with us."

Keeping me fully engaged, the angel continues. "Many ask *I AM* to give them a sign, a clear vision or signpost in front of them before they venture on. But when Moses asked *I AM* to show him His glory, *I AM* said He would cause His goodness to pass in front of Moses. *I AM* then told Moses he could not see His face, for no one may see Him and live."

"You're right" I add, feeling a bit silly telling the angel who is speaking Papa God's message that he is correct. "Like Moses, we are not able to see ahead what pathway Papa God is taking, but we can see where he has been. That's a powerful assurance to know that God is indisputably as good as His word! All He does and speaks is truth."

Our conversation continues as the angelic form compassionately speaks. "Yes, the presence of *I AM* directs you, then guides you to your daily destination. Many assume they are in the driver's seat, determined to arrive at their target point through their own effort. They are not fully aware *I AM* is the driver and they are the transported vehicles. Sometimes there are detours on the path which the driver needs to take. When you are in the trailered car viewing out the window, you notice the unusual terrain and often experience a bumpy ride. But the detour ends, and the intended station is reached."

"It's stress free and resting in Him that way, isn't it?" I interject.

He gently speaks. "*I AM* will teach you and instruct you in the way which you should go. He will counsel you with His eye upon you. This is the trust you have in *I AM*. Trust is the foundation and security of knowing *I AM*, your ever-present guide in life."

"It's a profound message confirming Papa God's loving care of His beloved. We need this reminder often," I add.

Contemplating the humor of my next comment, I blurt out "So we probably shouldn't say Jesus take the wheel."

"He already has" he adds.

Starting to thank him and ask his name, I turn to face him directly, but unexpectedly he is gone.

I assume he is behind us riding in the white car on the top row of the transporter.

"For this God is our God forever and ever. He will be our guide even to the end" (Psalm 48:14 NIV).

"We can make our plans, but the Lord determines our steps"
(Proverbs 16:9 NLT).

"The Lord directs the steps of the godly. He delights in every detail of their lives. Though they stumble, they will never fail, for the Lord holds them by the hand"
(Psalm 37:23-24 NLT).

Points to Ponder

- Do you find it odd that Papa God would have an angel be silly to get a clear, concise message to us? Journal your thoughts.

- Is it a new concept for you to think of Jesus as your driver and to trust Him to take you safely to your intended destination? Have you experienced the stress-free pleasure of resting in Him that way?

Prayer

Papa God, teach and instruct me in the way I should go. Counsel me and watch over me. I trust You, Jesus, as the driver of my life and I know You will get me safely to my intended destination.

Sparkling Lights

We have completed our move into a new home. Sitting and thanking God for the adventure of being in a new environment, we notice sparkling lights permeating the room we are in. They remind me of fireflies in the evening. I get up to attempt to take a closer look, and they seem to congregate around me. Some of the lights change color, turning to a brilliant blue. Many have become a soft hue of orange, while others remain a brilliant white. I react with amazement, feeling the sparkling lights are dancing before us intertwined with expressions of joy.

Holy Spirit tells me these lights radiating the glory of the Throne Room are heavenly angels of hope, comfort, wisdom and joy. They have been sent by God to assure us He knows the good plans He has for us here in our new home.

What delight to see these lights filling the room with the warmth and sweetness of heaven. We thank God for His perfect homecoming gift to us.

"Every good and perfect gift is from above, coming down from the Father of heavenly lights, who does not change like shifting shadows"
(James 1:17 NIV).

"For I know the plans I have for you, says the Lord. They are plans for good and not for disaster, to give you a future and a hope"
(Jeremiah 29:11 NLT).

Points to Ponder

- Do you see the divine radiance of the lights of God's angels in your home? Workplace?

- Has God given you a "homecoming" gift like this before?

Prayer

Father God, I adore You. Bless me to know Your goodness, holiness, perfection and love that never ceases. Father, allow Your heavenly lights to burn eternally bright all around me.

ENCOUNTER

Earthquake

My husband, our granddaughter, and I have just come home from a morning walk. We begin to play a ball game in the family room when the news comes on about an earthquake in Alaska.

I want to continue to play the game with our granddaughter, but my legs become extremely weak. Thinking they are going to give out on me, I hang on to the side of the closest chair.

What's going on, Jesus? I haven't prayed for the people affected by the earthquake yet. Everything is happening so fast. I feel my feet leave the floor. Quickly I am lifted up off the flooring. As I feel myself rising higher an angel meets me in the air and gently, but firmly takes hold of my hand. Looking down at the scene that swiftly appears below us, I realize we are hovering high above major gridlock on a snowy highway. Without the angel saying anything, I understand that people are trying to navigate out of the center of Anchorage, Alaska, to escape earthquake damage.

Simultaneously, still hovering over the highway, the angel and I are guided to reach down and pluck up cars with drivers and passengers in them. Being able to hold each individual car is strange. All are the size of the small toy cars my grandsons play with. I can see the occupants inside their vehicles and hear voices frantically praying. "Jesus! Jesus!" Some are only able, in fear or confidence, to call out the name of Jesus. With awesome amazement, and God's angel watching, I thank Jesus that these are the cars I am rerouting. Divine, supernatural help is responding to the Name of Jesus.

We set the cars on alternative routes out of the city, removed from the congested highway. Traffic is balanced, and cars are moving freely.

Our mission is over. I am back home. Only seconds in natural time have passed. I'm still holding onto the chair, standing next to my granddaughter. She keeps saying "earthquake, Grandma." "Yes, baby girl, we'll pray for the safety of all the people."

The day this happened, I didn't react to the news by asking Papa God to send me. I didn't even ask if I could help. My focus was to share playtime with my granddaughter. Jesus loves our special relationship with Him. He knows we are willing and ready to co-labor with Christ through whatever means He chooses.

"For we are God's masterpiece. He has created us anew in Christ Jesus, so we can do the good things He planned for us long ago"
(Ephesians 2:10 NLT).

"For it is God who works in you, both to will and to work for His good pleasure"
(Philippians 2:13 ESV).

"For God is not unjust so as to overlook your work and the love that you have shown for His name in serving the saints, as you still do"
(Hebrews 6:10 ESV).

Points to Ponder

- There will always be someone in need. How can you help getting them through life's obstacles?
- Think of gestures you have done that seem insignificant to you but are huge to someone you helped. Journal using these two questions.
- Have you experienced the absence of time? Explain.

Prayer

Papa God, forgive me for the times when I seem distracted and focused on other things. I want to co-labor with You. Cause me to be sensitive to prayer needs and help me to respond to Your call.

ENCOUNTER

Beauty Or Deception

An angel takes my hand and we are immediately on a crowded street. There are many skyscraper buildings, and the streets are bustling with people. I know I have been here before. It seems to be an Americanized city overseas, but I can't yet identify it.

As we stand on the street he points to a peacock. The peacock is definitely out of place in this setting. It is fanning its tail and people begin to point to the bird and grab others so they can see his exquisite beauty. I am captivated by the colors in his tail. I comment to the angel how pretty I think the bird is. Surprisingly he shakes his head and I understand that through seeing this bird I am being shown that what appears to be good and lovely often is not.

The angel then carries us to a beach. We walk along the shore spotting many peacocks once again out of place. Peacock feathers are everywhere. A male peacock is fanning his tail. The angel, who I know is an angel of wisdom, communicates with me that these birds represent over-confidence, pride, and vanity.

I tremble because I think he is showing me the peacock and calling me prideful. I ask God for forgiveness. He shakes his head. *"As far as the east is from the west, so far has He already removed our transgressions from us."* (Psalm 103:12 NIV). "But be aware. Among you are people of arrogance and haughtiness. They will try to draw as many as possible into their flock with their flamboyant appearance and mannerisms."

We are then transported together to a trail in a forest. Peacocks emerge from everywhere. Feathers are flying in the wind. We begin walking the trail. I have the feeling I'm becoming confined. Peacocks are behind each tree. Eyes are looking at me. I can hear their call. "Look at me! Look at my beauty! Come to me!"

Closing my eyes in an attempt to dismiss what I see and hear, the angel states emphatically, "I want you to see this for the children's sake." "What children?" I respond. "The ones you have been loving and praying for."

Holy Spirit allows me to recognize what a strong pull deception has and how it appears before God's children of all ages, attempting to draw them in. This deception manipulation must be stopped.

My heart breaks. "They are unsuspecting! They are so naive! The young ones are so easily tricked and trusting. They are unwary and easily preyed upon."

"Lord God, how can I pray?" The angelic messenger responds with words from God's Throne. "You've been called to pray for hedges of protection to surround the children. Pray that babies and toddlers will live in safety, and for wholeness to return to each victimized child. Pray for an awakening in the Body of Christ to know their identity and power of *I AM* within themselves. Speak with your supernatural divine power for the covered and hidden things to be exposed, for fear to be replaced by its opposite, LOVE! Pray also for repentance and the washing of the blood of the Lamb for the perpetrators."

As I begin to pray right then and there, I release freedom by the power of the Name of Jesus to those children and adults that have been brought into deception and lies. Children of varied ages who had been successfully hidden begin to come out and be seen from behind the trees and peacocks. I attempt to count the numbers, but am unable to keep up with so many appearing.

The process then begins of telling them how valuable and loved they are by Jesus and by us. Peace guards the hearts and minds of those who once had none.

"And the peace of God, which surpasses all understanding, will guard your hearts and your minds in Christ Jesus"
(Philippians 4:7 ESV).

We feed them, not only food for their bodies, but food for their spirits. With intense passion and love we continue to speak of their immense value.

I return with the angel to my home, but he ceases to be visible. I stay up praying for the rest of the night feeling what he had showed me is of the utmost importance to Father God's heart. God sent His angel to show the example of the beautiful peacock bird, but how deception is rampant and comes in various forms. We have the privilege of joining with our victorious Lord to co-labor with Him and protect the young ones, bringing His light to shine on the deep darkness.

"Take no part in the worthless deeds of evil and darkness; instead, expose them"
(Ephesians 5:11-12 NKJV).

"See that you do not despise one of these little ones. For I tell you that in heaven their angels always see the face of my Father who is in heaven"
(Matthew 18:10 ESV).

"But their evil intentions will be exposed when the light shines on them"
(Ephesians 5:13 NLT).

Points to Ponder

- How can you practically co-labor with Jesus to protect the young ones?
- What can you do to bring His Light to shine on the deep darkness?
- Are you able to intercede (to prayerfully labor fervently, to travail, to weep) for those entangled in deception?

Prayer

Jesus, I thank You for Your hand of protection. I ask You to guard the young ones from harm, holding them securely as they rest between Your shoulders. May I be Your praying servant on behalf of unsuspecting children and adults, causing Your light to shine and dissipate the deep darkness.

SMALL SIGHTINGS

Purity Plane

Sitting in the warm summer evening with friends is a soothing place to discuss how exciting this life with Jesus is. Movement above us catches my eye. What is up there that we are about to see? Walking slowly in a circle above us are a few of the prophets of old, suspended above the trees. They are encircling us in mid-air, not saying anything. All are dressed in long robes of white and are walking in a deliberate, slow-motion pace.

A small airplane flies back and forth at low altitude overhead but abruptly changes its direction as it approaches the prophets. It's as if the pilot is cautioned by an angelic force to avoid an unseen disturbance in the atmosphere.

We're sure they can hear us discussing the times when the prophets in God's word were called by God mightily to demonstrate signs, wonders, and miracles. A supernatural hush came over each of us as Holy Spirit speaks to us. "Understand that the prophets have walked where you are walking. Father God was pleased with them.

"Father God is raising you to a new plane of revelation. He calls it the Purity Plane. Do not be afraid or startled by His words. Your mind shifts to thinking you are not pure. But Father sees your passion for Jesus as a pure plumb line, not wavering from one side to another.

"The Cloud of Witnesses are surrounding and urgently summoning you. As they do, Father pulls you up to the plumb line of His purity where revelation will astound you. Come up! It is a new level. Set your feet where Jesus takes you higher. His loving desire for you is to comprehend more of Himself."

The prophets circle one more time and begin to ascend. All rapidly become out of sight.

"Blessed are the pure in heart, for they will see God"
(Matthew 5:8 NIV).

"Finally, brothers and sisters, whatever is true, whatever is noble, whatever is right, whatever is pure, whatever is lovely, whatever is admirable – if anything is excellent or praiseworthy – think about such things"
(Philippians 4:8 NIV).

"Create in me a pure heart, O God, and renew a steadfast spirit within me"
(Psalm 51:10 NIV).

Deeper Revelation

Holy Spirit's words "The prophets have walked where you are walking" speaks to us that they had a starting point also. They progressed as we are, continuing to gain more knowledge and understanding, and growing in our relationship with Jesus. We desire to be close to Papa God, close in His Presence. We desire to be a stream of love to Jesus, to one another and to the world around us. As we are close to Him, we are like a stream that is the purest close to its source. Jesus is our source. We pursue to live a life that honors God.

Only a moment had passed when we heard the gentle sound of a large swarm of dragonflies. We watched them hover, then dip and circle high, then dip again. Not knowing if the dragonflies are connected to the appearance of the prophets, we looked up the meaning of dragonflies. Dragonflies symbolize long overdue changes and transformation. It seems too coincidental.

Points to Ponder

- Can you name someone who may have told you they have walked where you are walking in your spiritual relationship with Jesus?

- How did they identify their walk?

- What hinders you from desiring to be raised up to a new plane of revelation?

Prayer

Heavenly Father God, raise me up to the plumb line of Your purity where Your revelation will astound me. I long to come up to a new plain. Set my feet where Jesus can take me higher. Allow me to comprehend Your loving desire for me.

ENCOUNTER

Where's The Precision?

Sitting in a chair with my feet up is my favorite position for reading. "Hello." Someone greets me before I get a page opened in my book. I look up and see standing before me an angelic figure which appears to be the conductor of a band. "Let's go," I hear. A group of angels each with musical instruments in the ready position are in front of my chair. The conductor angel taps on my chair twice, sweeps his arms upward then down quickly and the instruments shockingly begin to screech, blare, and blast unpleasant noise into my room. He then gives the command to march. Some angels went sideways, some backwards, many shuffle, some skipped and some stood still. The conductor tapped my chair and asked me if I thought the band of angels were out of sync with each other.

"Yes! Absolutely!" I certainly agreed with the phrase out-of-sync. "What is all this" I asked the conductor angel. His reply startled me. "The church is out of sync with the calendar of *I AM*." I was not expecting that kind of an answer. I remembered studying God's calendar and the scripture in Genesis 1." *"Then God said, 'Let lights appear in the sky to separate the day from the night. Let them be signs to mark the seasons, days, and years. Let these lights in the sky shine down on the earth.' And that is what happened. God made two great lights—the larger one to govern the day, and the smaller one to govern the night. He also made the stars"* (Genesis 1:14-16 NLT). I read from the Psalms also.

"He made the moon to mark the seasons, and the sun knows when to go down" (Psalm 104:19 NIV).

Conductor angel tells me the calendar of *I AM* determines the time and the feast days. "I do know that from my studies. The Christian church is not in uniformity with the rhythm of the seasons because we follow the Roman or Gregorian calendar." I do recall studying that in God's calendar every month begins with the first visible crescent moon, or the first light.

"Be knowledgeable" Conductor Angel declares. He picks up my Bible off the table next to me, and turns to Leviticus 23. Handing me the Bible, I read in verse 2 *"These are the Lord's appointed festivals"* (Leviticus 23:2 NIV).

"Be knowledgeable, be informed. Know the Calendar of *I AM* and His timing," Conductor Angel repeats. "The calendar of *I AM* is eternal" God's messenger adds, sweeping his arms upward then down quickly again. Responding to their conductor's direction, the angel band picks up their instruments, begin playing a musical piece with a strong pulsating beat and marches off in perfect precision. Be knowledgeable. Those words ring true in my ear.

Points to Ponder

- Have you studied God's calendar?
- Are you aware of His seven feasts during the year?
- What comes to your mind as you compare various calendars with God's calendar.

Prayer

Father God, help me to be more knowledgeable of Your calendar. I desire to know and discern the times, seasons, and understand the full meaning of Your feasts.

ENCOUNTER

Extreme

My husband and I spent a few days visiting our son and his family. After a fun, invigorating day with the grandchildren and their parents, we said goodnight to all and headed to bed for much-needed sleep. My thoughts turned to being incredibly grateful to Jesus for blessing us with such wonderful children and grandchildren. My heart exploded with love and thanksgiving to Jesus. My life is exciting, and often adventurous living with Jesus!

As I was lying in bed, worshiping Jesus, and reflecting on His word and the goodness of God's love for me, I noticed movement at the foot of the bed. Startled and alarmed, I saw an angel standing at the foot of the bed. He was dressed in a man's dark suit, standing very stately and was looking right at me. Abruptly sitting straight up, I loudly exclaimed to him, "Your name is EXTREME!!"

Did I wake up the entire household? No one stirred from their sleep. The angel nodded at me in agreement, gave me a soft smile and said, "I'll be working with you. You will understand my name." I strained my eyes to see him, but he was gone as quickly as he had shown up.

"Do not neglect hospitality to strangers, for by this some have entertained angels without knowing it"
(Hebrews 12:2 NASB).

"I, therefore, the prisoner of the Lord, beseech you to walk worthy of the calling with which you were called"
(Ephesians 4:1 NIV).

Deeper Revelation

I've had quite a few encounters and interactions with angels. Usually, I understand the purpose of their angelic visitations, but this one was different. I was overwhelmed and curious at his quick appearance and the words he spoke.

According to Webster's dictionary, "extreme" means "being far from the norm." Yes, this angel called EXTREME was far from the norm. He was much larger and appeared much stronger to the utmost degree than others I have seen.

I was hopeful that EXTREME would return to inform or advise me more. But I was not able to comprehend what these extreme capacities might be. Extreme healing? Extreme evangelizing? Extreme Loving? Extreme ground plowing? Extreme intercession?

I had become very watchful, anticipating his return.

Points to Ponder

- Think of extreme conditions that God may be preparing you for. What are they?

- Is He giving you spiritual tools to use? Describe.

- Are the tools for current use?

- What are your emotions when thinking of extreme conditions?

Prayer

Lord God, allow me to partner with You and Your angelic beings to live an exciting and adventurous life with Jesus!

ENCOUNTER

The Angel Extreme Again

I was asked if I had encountered the angel EXTREME again. When I contemplated his words from the first time I met him, "I'll be working with you, you will understand my name" I became curious if God wanted him to appear and bring clarity to His message.

My thought had briefly passed through my mind when I heard a voice say, "Here you go." and looked up to see EXTREME. He handed me a pair of night vision goggles. As I accepted the goggles, I understood the goggles are able to bring visibility beyond what a human being's natural vision picks up. EXTREME's presence seemed to bring a sudden revelation from Father God that imaging can show where an area has been disturbed or changed. Changed how? Was I going to be involved in an investigative activity?

I received a gas mask and an air tank from him, which made me fairly nervous. I've seen combat pictures. I understand what a gas mask and an air tank represent in those pictures. The angel calmly responded to my fear. "The dust will be thick. But then the air will be clean. Things will be brought to the forefront. Forgiveness will be a reality. Love will be strong. You'll be taken care of" he declared.

Those words were resonating in my spirit. I waited to hear more from EXTREME, but he had departed.

Our good, good Father God will bring us His love, rest, and peace and the supernatural operation of Holy Spirit.

"When anxiety was great within me, Your consolation brought me joy"
(Psalm 94:19 NIV).

"For God has not given us a spirit of fear and timidity, but of power, love and self-discipline"
(2 Timothy 1:7 NLT).

"For we wrestle not against flesh and blood, but against principalities, against powers, against the rulers of the darkness of this world, against spiritual wickedness in high places"
(Ephesians 6:12 KJV).

"Arise, shine, for your light has come! And the glory of the Lord is risen upon you. For behold, the darkness shall cover the earth, and deep darkness the people; but the Lord will arise over you, and His glory will be seen upon you"
Isaiah 60:1-2 (NKJV).

Deeper Revelation

I contemplated his next assignment with me. Possibly the next time he would stay longer. His visit stirred me because I believe the angel named EXTREME was indicating that we, as a society or the world, would be seeing extreme degrees of events, misunderstood situations, and circumstances in the coming days and years.

Points to Ponder

- Imagine possible scenarios where you may need a gas mask or night vision goggles.

- If the angel named EXTREME appeared to you today, would you be ready and willing to join him in whatever adventure he was inviting you into?

Prayer

Papa God, help me be willing to partner with the angel EXTREME and adventure with You. Stir me to actively read Your Word. I know that You speak to me and show me what I must do to be ready.

SMALL SIGHTINGS

Angelic Walls

There are thousands upon thousands, and ten thousand times ten thousand angels around God's throne. There are uncountable myriads of angels everywhere. Often quite a few of them will appear together before the six of us Jesus-loving people who were desiring to spend time in the presence of Jesus. As we opened in prayer and worship, the walls in the room seemed to have movement to them. What an odd thing to see. I continued to look closely at the walls and clearly saw that the walls were completely full of angels. Horizontal lines of angels upon lines of heavenly messengers from wall to wall, floor to ceiling, corner to corner, horizontal lines of angels on top of the lines below. This pattern of angels repeated until every wall in the room was filled. It was not a painting on wallpaper, or photographs of angels besides photographs. These were God's live, angelic beings covering every section of the structured walls enclosing us.

"Why are they here?" I asked Papa God. One angel stepped forward. "We are your walls of protection" he described, "your shelter, your barrier while you are here." I needed to grasp the vastness of this 360-degree wall again. The angels were tightly pushed against each other. No room was given for an intruder to enter.

I've read that in times of Old Testament war, when the enemy assaulted and left gaps in the city walls, that leaders would defend their city by standing in the areas of broken walls to protect their people.

"Do we have forces wanting to combat or discouraged us?" I asked God's angel. "*I AM* is using us to keep you from doubt, discouragement, or defeat while you are here. He created within each of you a power of understanding when words and visuals are combined. Seeing angels here establishes a true belief within you that we have assignments from *I AM* concerning you."

"It's awesome! Look!" I called to the friends gathered. "Can you see our angelic wall of protection tonight?"

Declarations of thanksgiving erupted in the room.

"I see them! They are everywhere!" The five friends each began to define what was in their sight.

"Try counting the number of them!"

"This is almost unreal!"

"They are so close together!"

"None have wings that I can see!"

"No, I don't see wings either!"

"They are a battalion of angels!"

"Thank you, Jesus for sending Your angels!"

I lifted my thanks to God as our holy worship ascended into the His Throne Room. We became aligned with heaven. All angels in the room united with us in one glorious, harmonious song, worshiping and exalting the One True God.

What an extraordinary, magnificent night we had being filled with the presence of Jesus. We stayed tightly knit together with Him and each other long past the first few hours of the morning.

"He who dwells in the shelter of the Most High will abide in the shadow of the Almighty. I will say to the Lord, 'My refuge and my fortress, my God in whom I trust"
(Psalm 91:1-2 ESV).

"The angel of the Lord encamps around those who fear him, and he delivers them"
(Psalm 34:7 ESV).

Points to Ponder

- Why do you suppose the angels covered every section of the enclosing walls? Consider all reasons, practical and spiritual.
- Read Psalms 91. Can you see how God has assigned angles to watch over you and protect you?
- What stands out to you most when reading Psalm 91?

Prayer

Thank You Father God that Your angels watch over me with protection and might. Thank You that they are encamped completely around me because of the depth of Your love. I know I am Your cherished one.

ENCOUNTER

A Bonfire?

The total of every published Facebook post, all in paper form, are burning in a towering bonfire. People are scrambling trying to read pages of posts before they disintegrate. Grabbing literal pages that have not yet burned, they check the posts to see if they desire to read each, and throw them back into the fire if they do not.

Writers of posts are sobbing in pain, grieving to see what they perceive as their outstanding work being burned up, knowing what they confidently posted has not been read by the entirety of readers.

As this huge crowd of stunned people stand around the bonfire wailing in disbelief, the fire dies down to only black ashes and a few embers. Bits of white paper are sticking up out of the ashes. Angels are pulling some, but not all, of the charred papers out of the cinders. The few they have retrieved are the pure posts without mixture that Papa God is allowing to be read.

Angels one by one lay the papers carefully on the ground. Authors frantically try to find the ones they composed. When theirs are nowhere to be found they sob uncontrollably.

Unexpectedly a large, commanding angel appears standing over the scattered ashes. A hush falls over the crowd. He raises his voice and exclaims "what you write becomes your identity. *I AM* has burned your false identity. Understand that your meditation has the power to determine your identity. Are you meditating on *I AM* and your righteousness in Him because of Christ? WHO is your reason for posting?"

These seem to be harsh words, but then he gently adds "Know that *I AM* sees you as He sees Jesus. You need not prove yourself. You are loved. You are strong. You are His."

Some shake their heads and walk away, not comprehending his message. Many stay to read pure untainted posts. The angel has disappeared from sight. I didn't see him leave.

Papa God wants us to know our identity is in Him!

"Since we are his children, we are his heirs. In fact, together with Christ we are heirs of God's glory"
(Romans 8:17 NLT).

"Anyone who belongs to Christ has become a new person. The old life is gone; a new life has begun"
(2 Corinthians 5:17 NLT).

"Whatever you do, work at it with all your heart, as working for the Lord, not for human masters, since you know that you will receive an inheritance"
(Colossians 3:23-24 NIV).

Points to Ponder

- If you frequently write and post on a social media platform, who and what is your reason for doing so?

- We know our identity is to be rooted in Christ However, there are times when we need to invite God to examine our hearts and motives. Invite Him to do so now, and journal what He reveals to you.

- Specifically ask Him if there is any place where your identity is rooted in something other than Him.

Prayer

Father God, Papa God, I want my identity to be firmly rooted and grounded in You and You alone. I ask that you examine me and show me any place in my heart, mind, and emotions where my identity is not rooted in You

ENCOUNTER

Delicious Pears

Standing in the middle of a congested metropolitan city block, I notice people walking quickly, taking long strides, determined to get someplace fast. Cars, buses, bicycles, and taxis all are transporting people to unknown destinations. Commotion is everywhere. The blaring sound of car horns screaming their obscenities to other drivers is intense. A constant honking to wake-up motorists unaware of the immediate opportunity to change lanes causes me to express annoyance, at least to myself. Long lines of vehicles jammed together form an unsightly serpentine appearance.

My soul is agitated by the noise and turbulent motion. I lift my head and look up. Our brilliant sun is surrounded by a clear sapphire blue sky. Lovely rays of warmth are streaming down from this earth's sun. It isn't disturbed by the disorder I sense.

Wanting to be absorbed into a still, calm, peaceful environment, I call out to Papa God. "Take me into the sanctuary of Your Presence."

As I express my need to Papa God, He sends an angel who places me on the outside of a beautiful garden which encompasses an entire city block. The garden is surrounded by a high, decorative wrought iron fence. I can see and still hear the commotion of the traffic encircling me but the beauty of what I see beyond the fence is surreal. The hush of the exquisite beauty silences all distractions, and I am drawn in. Colorful carpets of yellow, orange, gold, lavender, pink and white flowers line its border. Hues of green in the grasses, shrubs, and plants bring comfort and relief to my weary eyes. This astonishing garden is an oasis and a safe haven allowing me to step away from the rush and into the serenity of Papa's creation.

Surprisingly I see in the center of the garden a pear tree, loaded with huge perfect pears. The pears are so numerous that the branches holding them are weighted down, almost to the ground. As I study this magnificent tree, I feel the taste buds in my mouth begin to work overtime. All I can think of is how much I desire some of that fruit. I know it is going to be so sweet, so satisfying. The longing to taste the fruit is almost more than I can bear. Desperation comes over me and I find myself saying "I need to plan a way to get past the fence, to the interior of the garden, and to the tree."

The angel who brought me here has an expression of amusement on his face that makes me wonder what will happen.

People are walking the circumference of the garden. No one seems to realize there is a tree in the center of this cultivated piece of land. The individuals appear to be preoccupied with the dealings in their personal lives. I stop a passer-by and ask him, "Sir, how do I get inside the garden and get some of that fruit?" He turns his head to see the tree as if for the first time. He replies "Oh! A tree! Well, rent a ladder and climb over the fence."

"Thank you," I tell him and proceed to find a place that rents ladders. I drag a twelve-foot ladder to the fence and set it up to climb over the high fence. My mind is surveying the situation. How will I be able to get down on the other side? The fence must be at least fourteen feet high. The urge to have a taste of succulent pears is becoming more intense. I can hardly cope with the insatiable craving I have for the fruit of this particular tree. I set the ladder aside. The angel is watching me with curiosity.

Another walker approaches me. "Excuse me. How do I get into that garden so I can have some pears?" He catches sight of the tree with surprise and advises me. "Get a tree digger and uproot the tree. Then you will have to rent a hauling truck and have the tree pulled over to the edge of the garden."

After a few hours of checking various tree removal service companies, I find one that will help me with my dilemma. I explain to them that my request is quite extreme, but I am willing to pay the price just to get at the fruit of the tree.

I know this is my tree which has been wooing me to taste its fruit since I first discovered it in the garden.

Arriving at the garden, the company sets their equipment on stilts enabling it to be used over the fence. To my surprise the men are successful in uprooting the tree. The tree lays on its side. Pears begin to fall off the branches. This tree is immense! The roots are enormous.

The men from the tree service are shocked seeing the extraordinary size of the roots.

I thank the men and proceed to call a hauling truck company asking if they are able to move the tree against the fence. Soon, I say to myself, I will have the fruit which I longingly desire. As the tree is being dragged over towards me some of the massive branches stick through the fence.

Yes! The fruit of my tree! Thankfully I reach for a pear and begin to eat it. I had worked so hard planning ways to bring the tree to me. I proved I could receive the fruit. My efforts had actually paid off! The pear I taste is good, but it does not satisfy me. Disillusioned, I had longed to sit under the tree and eat to my heart's content.

The angel God sent, who has been with me and carefully watching all that I did to get to this tree, appears next to me and says, "Take one more look. *I AM* is giving you clarity." As he instructs me, I look and see the tree is back in the middle of the garden, straight and statuesque as I had first seen it, loaded with beautiful huge pears. There are no trucks, no diggers, no equipment blocking the beauty of my tree. It is illuminated in an indescribable light.

I feel this ministering angel take my hand and walk me along the fence line, around the garden. A sweet fragrance filled the air as we walk together, admiring my tree. "*I AM* delights in you," he whispers. The words flow freely from my mouth "and He loves that Jesus made a way for me to be with Him now and forever."

We walk a few more steps around the garden. The angel points. I glance towards the fence. There before me is an unlocked gate, beckoning me to come in! "I have been so busy attempting to get over the fence I never saw the gate." He smiles a heartwarming smile and gestures for me to approach the gate. As I do, without my help the gate opens to its fullest capacity. I walk straight to the tree.

My heart begins to dance with anticipation knowing the tree contains what I have been longing for. Graciously, ever so sweetly, the tree bends down, allowing me to effortlessly eat of its fruit. I don't even pick a pear off the tree but rather lean into it. As I touch the pear, it ripens from the inside out and I begin to eat. Delectable juice from the fruit is running down my face. I don't care. It is the richest, most nourishing fruit I have ever eaten! One pear would satisfy me, but the tree has embraced me, my spirit is rejoicing, and I continue to receive more of the continuous gift it offers.

The fragrant floral aroma displaces the unclean city air. I take deep breaths, filling my lungs. My emotions surface before my brain can identify what I am smelling. I am overwhelmed by LOVE Itself! Looking around, I notice a few others beginning to react to this fragrance also.

"Eat as much as you like," the angel suggests. "Yes," I respond. "I feel silly having exerted such physical and mental energy to approach the tree."

"Listen to the voice you hear!" The angel touches my ear. Holy Spirit speaks to my spirit. "You are tasting and seeing God is a good Father. As you share your experience, and you will, it will become a parable to those hearing. You tried the plans of man. You were striving, wanting to prove you are worthy of receiving the fruit. Man's plan and efforts do not bring you to Jesus Christ, the Tree of Life with the satisfaction of His pure, unconditional love. No matter how each man, woman, or child feels about him or herself, Father's arms are outstretched for all to come to Him through His Son. He tells them they are worthy, honored, and loved.

My face is covered with sweet juice. I excitedly share with the angel beside me "Papa God brought me to the sanctuary of His Presence as I called out to Him. He has been here with me this entire time and sent you, His serving angel, to lead me to the open gate."

I see the angel nodding in agreement as Holy Spirit gently says "Now go, share, and tell others to do the same. Blessed are those who hunger and thirst for righteousness, for they will be filled." There are countless numbers of people walking past the tree waiting to hear the parable you just lived. Let them know Jesus, the Tree of Life, never fails to bear fruit. He is true fulfillment."

I gather as many pears as I can hold and run outside the gate. Passing out pears to anyone who will accept them, I encourage my new friends to come in, discover the magnificent tree as I did, and eat of its fruit. It is evident there is refreshment as they approach the tree. Soon more curious ones join, and the gathering becomes very large. A calm sense of wonder supersedes the disorder that is outside the garden. People sit on the lush grass, looking at me with expectation, waiting to hear what I have to say.

Holy Spirit speaks through me as I begin to share my experience of the magnificent, and glorious Tree of Life that belongs to all. Hearts are opening to the Father's unconditional love. Jesus Christ, the Tree of Life is drawing them into an everlasting, abundant life which is theirs through Him. I see joy and peace on every face as He calls each one His Beloved.

Songs of angels rejoicing permeate the atmosphere. The angel gives my shoulder a squeeze and ecstatically declares "The Family of God is growing!" There is a visible splendor of angels and the cloud of witnesses who have been waiting for this moment. They react with exuberant celebration and glorious, audible exaltation of the King of Kings. *"Holy, Holy, Holy is the Lord Almighty; the whole earth is full of His glory"* (Isaiah 6:3 KJV). I listen with thankfulness in my heart. Indeed, the whole earth is full of His Glory!

"For He satisfies the longing soul, and fills the hungry soul with goodness"
(Psalm 107:9 NKJV).

"For you shall go out in joy and be led forth in peace, the mountains and the hills before you shall break forth into singing and all the trees of the field shall clap their hands"
(Isaiah 55:12 ESV).

"Taste and see that the Lord is good; blessed is the one who takes refuge in Him"
(Psalm 34:8 NIV).

Points to Ponder

- Name someone who displays an exuberant celebration when realizing someone they know has come into a loving relation ship with Jesus Christ and is born again.

- Have there often been times when you just want to get away from the chaos?

- Has God taken you to a the sanctuary of His presence with Him? Journal about it.

Prayer

Papa God, may I, Your treasured one know the inner sweetness of Your Presence and have the satisfying knowledge of being with You.

ENCOUNTER

Conference Healing

Often God sends His angels to assist Him in spiritual, emotional, and physical healing at conferences. I was an invited speaker for an out of state church gathering, called to speak on God, our source of supernatural healing. I explained that the Bible is filled with times when God has sent an angel or angels to assist in His supernatural healing. I shared with the people seated in the pews and was aware that an expectancy had been stirred within them. My sight was drawn to the space behind the last row of pews. I saw 15 angels, five across, three rows deep standing alert in anticipation. They had been attentively listening to me talk about them, as if they were waiting for specific words to come out of my mouth. I felt a nudge from Holy Spirit and asked anyone who needed a healing touch from God to please stand. People all over the congregation rose. The moment individuals were standing, the angels responded to the command of God, traversing the pews, ministering to each one needing a healing touch from God. Papa God desires to reach people needing healing and does so often through His ministering angels ready to assist.

I remained silent, not needing to add any extra words as I watched from the platform. God was answering the cry of the people's hearts *"Heal me, Lord, and I will be healed"* (Jeremiah 17:14 NIV).

Physical manifestations, the external evidence of God's power of healing, were evident throughout the room. We were in the presence of Almighty God and His serving angels. God was doing His thing! He had dispatched His angels and they had carried out the intended assignment of God. Amazing testimonies came forth of God's creative miracles through physical, spiritual and emotional healing.

"He sent His word and healed them, and delivered them from their destructions (Psalm 107:20 NKJV).

"Lord my God, I called to You for help, and You healed me"
(Psalm 30:2 NIV).

Points to Ponder

- Have you been in a gathering where many people were receiving the healing touch of God?
- What thoughts came to your mind as you witnessed a sovereign act of God.
- What emotions surfaced?

Prayer

Father God, allow me to sense and know when You send Your angels to assist in spiritual, emotional, and physical healing. I want to be in Your presence to serve and help any way I can for whomever You want to touch. Thank you for allowing me to participate in Your creative miracles.

Strength For A Heart

I received a call asking for prayer for a hospitalized mother whose heart was not strong enough to pump the required blood throughout her body. God showed me in a vision two angels, one on either side of her hospital bed, each taking a side of her heart and lifting it as one would lift a barbell. Up and down, up and down. We knew that barbells increase strength and I expressed that even though the vision was unusual, it must be that the angels they were strengthening her heart. We prayed the vision, believing the word of God and expecting her recovery. The mother's heart indeed was strengthened and began functioning again as Jesus intended.

"Then said the Lord to me, 'you have seen well, for I am alert and active, watching over My word to perform it"
(Jeremiah 1:12 AMP).

"Bless the Lord oh my soul and forget not all His benefits. Who forgives all your iniquities, who heals all your diseases"
(Psalm 103:2-3 NKJV).

"Are not all angels ministering spirits sent to serve those who will inherit salvation"
(Hebrews 1:14 NIV).

Deeper Revelation

Even when things can't be explained in the natural as God is using His angels, there is no need to dismiss what He is doing. Embrace the vision you are seeing! God is not subject to our limitations of His ways. He is subject to His word, and His angels carry out their assignments from God quickly, without delay.

Points to Ponder

- Have you ever put your human limitations onto God and what He can do?
- If so, are you able to step back and take a bigger look at God?
- Do you believe God will perform His word, honor your faith and reward you as you diligently seek Him?

Prayer

Forgive me Father for the times I may have dismissed what I could not explain in the natural. Help me to embrace without limitations whatever it is You want to do and accomplish.

ENCOUNTER

Together

The lyrics "There's a New Kid in Town" by the Eagles was playing in my head. What an odd song originally from the 1970's to pop into my mind. Oh well, I'll just keep singing the chorus with it. But as I sing, the lyrics spurred another thought. I should go and welcome the new neighbors that are moving in, and offer to help.

Getting into my car and heading the store to buy ingredients for a nice welcome lunch, I turned on the radio with an Oldies but Goodies station tuned in. Turning the volume up a bit to hear the song playing, I jumped back in the seat. "There's a new kid in town" was ringing loudly through the radio frequencies filling my car with the words. Can this really be? I asked myself, astonished at what I was hearing. "This is crazy confirmation" my inner voice screamed! Something in the air seemed familiar but peculiar at the same time. I glanced over at the empty front seat and observed God's angelic being, named Elyacaph, who took me around the world to see the bread lines of people desiring the touch of Jesus. Elyacaph was silent on the way home. He appeared to be hearing the next part of his assignment. I was curious if he would stay in my vehicle.

Lunch was prepared and arranged in a brightly colored basket containing the edibles, early blooming yellow flowers, some pretty napkins, and extra water bottles ready to be delivered. Time to drive over to the new neighbors, with Elyacaph accompanying me.

The sweet new couple was grateful for the basket of goodies and a reason to take a break from unpacking. "It is such a treat," they commented "to have you stop. We haven't had a homemade meal since we started packing to move."

Our first visit lasted quite a while. They were eager to share their plans to make the new home uniquely theirs. I found out they longed to move here to be close to family again. How wonderful it is to hear these heartwarming words.

Needing to let them have their lunch and continue their unpacking, I assured them we'd be connecting often. "Welcome to the neighborhood! We are delighted you are here and I am sure your family is thrilled you are close."

As I headed back to my home, I contemplated the many people we know who are also making major moves to return to extended families. It is more prevalent to hear these stories now, and an interesting reversal of the trend many years ago to move away. I could feel my eyes, lips, and spirit all smiling simultaneously. This is precisely why we made a move also.

What an uplifting morning. I'm happy for the newcomers, for them being reconnected with family again. My soul is filled with joy. Starting to clean up the dishes I used earlier I felt a warm hand on my shoulder. Turning, anticipating seeing my husband behind me, Elyacaph spoke invitingly "Come with me."

As he had before, he took my hand and we arrived at a home where a large number of people were together. "This one" Elyacaph whispered while I turned my head toward two people looking at each other, "this one speaking has a broken heart and is willing to repair the damage he has caused. He has come to the realization he needs to ask for forgiveness." The young man's emotions seemed neutral, changing to quietness, then to tears flowing as he expressed remorse. "I am responsible for your pain. I want to make it right with you. Please forgive me." With no hesitation, as if the other person had ceaselessly been waiting to hear those words, forgiveness is accepted, and hugs are shared. At that moment, a family was reconciled. Broad smiles have replaced concern on each person's face. There is an undeniable warmth emanating upward and outward from the home. "That's beautiful," I told Elyacaph. God's word says

"Make allowance for each other's faults, and forgive anyone who offends you. Remember the Lord forgave you, so you must forgive others."
(Colossians 3:13 NLT).

"There's more" Elyacaph indicated. He takes me with him to the other side of the world. My eyes focus on the widespread drought in the area. The land is void of crops. It appears to be a poorly developed, extremely impoverished country, yet people are living in this village. Many individuals emerge excitedly from small huts. I watch as a young man is greeted with open arms by a father. A woman and children come running from the hut. Crying, the woman embraces the young man who must be her son. Holy Spirit tells me their son was drawn as a lottery pick, educated in another country, and offered an academic research position at a university. But his heart longed to return to his native land and be with his family. His presence and expertise will cause the desperately needed building of hospitals, schools, homes in this village to begin.

The young man's father, walking with one arm wrapped tightly around his son's waist and his opposite hand sweeping in the air with excitement, leads the son into the hut. Dodging a few swarms of insects while attempting to keep up with father, the children raced to the hut to be included in the celebration. Mom came quickly behind, moving as swiftly as her tired legs could carry her. This mother takes pride in serving her family a meal of boiled insects, a few edible plants, and a fish that was caught by one of the children. She would sleep well tonight with her family together again.

Elyacaph then brings me into a large building with neatly kept landscaping and empty parking stalls outside. Inside we walk down dark, dismal halls, where drooping potted plants have been placed. I notice individual doors to private living quarters are open with a silent plea of "please, I am so lonely" reflecting off every ceiling, wall, and floor in what is now recognized as a home for the elderly. Sadness overtakes me. I must sit for a moment.

Down the hallway, the silent cries are muted by much commotion where a resident's door had been left open. Young children and their parents are filing into the resident's room. Soon slight sparkles of joy escape into the hallway and fill that section of the building. "We are happy to see you again, Dad. Are they taking good care of you? Is there anything you would like us to bring you next time? Nod if you can hear me, Dad. Oh, good. These are your grandchildren. They want to call you Grandpa," an adult voice declares. My sadness has been replaced by jubilation, realizing that a family had taken time to reunite with their loved one. The lonely individual's daily cry for family contact was heard. Soon laughter, spontaneous giggling, and upbeat cheerful conversations escape into the hallway filling that section of the building. The atmosphere is changed. There is light where there was darkness. Even the plant life has reacted and the plants are standing upright. God prompted the family to reunite with their loved one.

I ask Elyacaph if the residents have usual visitors and he replies "No. None. This place is not a home for the people here. It is a place where they live in loneliness without family contact. But change is coming."

"How?" I respond. A corner of my spirit begins to pick up sadness again, but from the other end of the hallway I hear laughter. "Let's go see" I beg Elyacaph. Right away, my feet were off the ground, and we observe one additional resident who is unable to contain herself through sobs of gratitude and joy. Her son or daughter had just arrived to be with her. Grandchildren gleefully were asking "Grandma, are you happy we are here? I brought my flute, Grandma. Do you want to hear me play it?" An airy, soft, melodic sound surrounded each person and filled the room. The sweet love of family overtook Grandma's sadness. Elyacaph spoke "her ordinary days of solitude became her richest day of blessing today."

Elyacaph motions that we are to move on. I hang on to him as we move speedily from one culture grouping of people to another. We slow down, hovering over sights of joyous wedding ceremonies, where the two families are coming together in celebration. Elyacaph and I witness births of a new generation into the family line of ecstatic parents and grandparents. We catch family victories of various kinds being celebrated, noting the strengthening of a sense of connection with all who are involved in these joyous festivities.

"Are you ready for another stop?" I was questioned. Elyacaph obviously is making sure I am aware of all that I need to see as he brings us to observe a mother and her three young children living their lives in hopelessness, pain and anger. These precious ones have been rejected by a husband and father who abandoned them. Bedtime routines are taking place. Whimpering cries of one of the children is her reminder the constant pain of an absent daddy. Wanting the pain to end and the child to drift off into the warmth of love, the mother says "find your favorite book and I will read it, sweetie." Fatiguing attempts to soothe her child while covering her own need to cry show on her countenance. "But Mommy, only Daddy reads this story to us. It is his favorite".

The evening is still young and the mother has done all she can to possibly make life ordinary for her children. "Why, God? Why? The children need him! I need him!" She seeks an answer from God. My messenger angel briefly points to the door. A soft rapping noise was coming from the front porch. The dog began to growl. "Who is it Mommy?" She moves to the door, opening it slightly to see the familiar face of her estranged husband.

"Daddy!" Came the cries of their three children racing to the door. "Daddy! We knew you'd come back! We knew it!" A wayward dad has made a crucial decision to return to his home and family.

"Thank you, Jesus for hearing my prayers" the mom speaks in a whisper. I caught a glimpse of Elyacaph nodding.

Suddenly we are moving again. I'm tightly holding on to Elyacaph. Are we in a hurry, I wonder? I feel if I were to let go of him, I would be falling from a high altitude faster than the speed of sound. Very briefly I am concerned, but Elyacaph pulls me closer to him and I remember this strong angel is sent to me by my Papa God to reveal His message.

We come to a high hill, able to watch lines of people vying for an opportunity to enter what appears to be a stadium. There must be a scheduled ballgame, meeting, or concert. Elyacaph indicates we are to stay and watch.

"Listen" said Elyacaph tilting his head. Earthly spaces surrounding us were filled with heavenly choir voices singing in unison. "All you need is love. Love is all you need."

"That's a Beatles song" I exclaimed. "What's with that?" I listened, perplexed, as a choir of countless voices from heaven were heard. Many people within the lengthy lines reacted and joined in. "All you need is love. Love is all you need."

"Is that a prelude to what is going on inside?"

"How true is this" Elyacaph comments. "These are the ones that know Jesus. All you need is the love of *I AM*, Jesus the Son, and Holy Spirit."

I watch as the lines of people become small groups with arms wrapped around one another. The groups enter the stadium, arm in arm as their voices become stronger. Small groups became larger until the entire stadium was filled to standing room only. "All you need is love" was contagiously being sung over and over by the masses inside and outside. Behavior and emotions are meshing. Unknowingly, "All you need is love!" has become the intended message to the people. No one attempted to disrupt what is happening by usurping the concert of raised voices. The atmosphere here is electrified.

Cars were parking blocks away. People are jumping out of their cars, racing breathlessly into the stadium. Soon there is no room for cars to park. Buses arrive, exit doors are opened with loud cheers from gratified passengers. The riders file off the buses and rush to engage with the tightly packed mass of people inside the stadium. "They are not yet aware that their desperation to be included in what is occurring is a holy call from *I AM*," Elyacaph explains.

"What is this? Why are you showing me all this, Elyacaph?" "*I AM* is giving you a symbolic picture of the greater meaning of what He is doing. He is revealing it first as your natural eyes are able to observe what is represented. Then your spiritual eyes will discern the fullness and fulfillment of His Kingdom plan in the spiritual realm. *I AM* always observes and maintains a proper order to bring about His perfection. This represents how *I AM* is calling His family back together. People are having their spirits opened to the love of Jesus."

Someone grabs a bullhorn and yells into it. "JESUS!" The crowd lets out a booming, reverberating roar of agreement. "All you need is the LOVE OF JESUS!" someone yells. An ear-piercing "YES AND AMEN!" echoes throughout the crowd.

I am able to see that unstoppable tears are filling the eyes of many. People are dropping to their knees, many are bowing, some are lying prostrate however they are able, and some remain standing. Arms are raised to the heavens. I hear multiple voices repeatedly proclaim "All I need is YOU, JESUS!"

"Remember your question of 'how'?" Elyacaph asks me. "This is how. This is the heart of *I AM*. The spiritual family of *I AM* is for eternity. Revival has hit! God's family is growing." The atmosphere is thick with united voices.

I'm compelled to proclaim these words to heaven. "God is love. He loves us all. His loving hand is drawing people into His family. It's the relationship of family that He has wanted since He created the world. People are experiencing the love of God and calling Him 'Abba', 'Daddy', 'Father'. His family is sharing the eternal inheritance we have because of Jesus, and the delight of dwelling in the perfect fellowship with the Lamb of God, Jesus Christ. God has ordained this loving relationship between Himself and His family to continue to grow and flourish for all of eternity!"

I thought I was sharing my thoughts with Elyacaph, but his assignment is over and he has faded from my sight.

Thank You, Papa God for sending Elyacaph again. His name means "God increases the family". Thank You for sending him and allowing me see these visible demonstrations of how deeply profound Your love of family is.

"The spiritual did not come first, but the natural, and after that the spiritual"
(1 Corinthians 15:46 NIV).

"For this reason, I kneel before the Father, from whom every family in heaven and on earth derives its name"
(Ephesians 3:14-15 NIV).

"God sets the lonely in families"
(Psalm 68:6 NIV).

"So then you are no longer strangers and aliens, but you are fellow citizens with the members of the household of God"
(Ephesians 2:19 ESV).

"God decided in advance to adopt us into His own family by bringing us to Himself through Jesus Christ. This is what He wanted to do, and it gave Him great pleasure"
(Ephesians 1:5 NLT).

Points to Ponder

- Have there been times when you heard a song and it confirmed what you believe God was telling you? Did you take action?

- Because of our salvation through Jesus Christ we become, along with all other believers, a valued, equal part of the single, eternal greatest spiritual family. Papa God is Abba, Father to all of humanity. We are His loved ones. Do you know Him?

- Have you witnessed the work of God calling families back together and/or into the family of God? Journal about your experience. Include as many details as possible.

Prayer

Papa God, thank You that I am adopted through Jesus Christ into Your own family. As Your beloved one I am called to be a blessing to other people and witness the growth of Your divine family. Thank You that Your love and power is released through me.

As I wrap up sharing this portion of my spiritual journey with you, a sweet, soft, untarnished new fragrance like a combination of honey, lavender, roses, apples, and lilies permeates my room. I am aware that it is a company of Papa God's angels who actively minister to us, are always around us, beside us and constantly with us. These angels are celebrating your time spent in these encounters, embracing the experiences. There is such extreme delight and joy in the air coming from the angels of God.

Are the angels dancing?.

"Day and night they never stop saying:

Holy, holy, holy is the Lord God Almighty,

who was, and is, and is to come. You are worthy

our Lord and God, to receive glory and honor

and power, for You created all things, and by

Your will they were created and have their being."

Amen.

(Revelation 4:8 NIV)

Margie Moormann's forte is being a bold risk-taker for God. She does not back off when He is directing her. She knows we are spirit beings living our lives in the spirit realm while in these bodies here on earth. Margie is rooted and grounded in Jesus the Vine. Wherever she is, Holy Spirit visions and heavenly angelic encounters abound.

Margie travels throughout the U.S. and across the world, speaking, teaching, prophesying, and being a facilitator for the Presence of God. She scripturally teaches one's true identity in Christ and that God has purposed, destined, and equipped each of us to live, see and co-labor with Jesus Christ in this supernatural life. She inspires all to realize their supernatural life is reality and that their own supernatural encounters await them. Her delightful sense of humor refreshes and fills mouths with laughter in the joy of the Lord.

Margie is a wife, mother, grandmother, sister, aunt, and friend who is passionately in love with God, Jesus Christ, and Holy Spirit. She is a member of Nebraska Christian Leaders Forum, is on the Nebraska State Team as Director of Leadership with Aglow International, leads bible studies in her church and community, and provides mentorship to her Christian "Living Beyond the Margins" individuals and groups.

Under the unction of Holy Spirit, Margie founded Papa God's Hide-away Ministries which has the mandate to be His light to the nations, bringing salvation to the ends of the earth. Lovers of Jesus and lovers of people come together in a family-style gathering to worship, share, fellowship, learn, grow and break bread together. Holy Spirit is the only keynote speaker at this free weekend gathering. Everyone present is honored as God's precious one and has a voice to share in God's anointed setting of spiritual flourishing.

To find out more information about Papa God's Hideaway Ministries visit the Facebook group page:

"The Promise ---Papa God's Hideaway."

Also available for teaching and sharing regarding the angelic realm check the Facebook group page:

"Angelic Stop Stations."

Margie can be reached at papagodshideaway@gmail.com.

Made in the USA
Coppell, TX
18 January 2023

11325890R00115